diabetic LIVING® Favorite Slow Cooker Recipes
VOLUME 1

DIABETIC LIVING® FAVORITE SLOW COOKER
RECIPES IS PART OF A BOOK SERIES
PUBLISHED BY BETTER HOMES AND GARDENS®
SPECIAL INTEREST MEDIA, DES MOINES, IOWA

Home-Style Chicken
and Noodles
recipe, page 13

Letter from the Editor

As a busy mom who works full-time, I know how challenging serving a wholesome meal can be. And because I have type 1 diabetes, eating nutritious food is important to help me control my blood sugars and feel good. That's why I am excited to share with you this new collection of healthful recipes, all of which use the popular 20th-century countertop appliance that's perfect for the 21st century—the slow cooker.

Using a slow cooker is an economical cooking method that saves both time and money. This awesome cooking vessel allows you to assemble a recipe in the morning and leave it alone all day. While you're busy doing other things, your meal simmers by itself, filling your home with the wonderful aroma of good food. At mealtime, your slow-cooked dish is ready to serve! To help you save money, you can use less-expensive meat cuts that reach optimum tenderness the longer they cook. And many of the recipes include make-ahead directions so that you prepare a dish or master recipe once and enjoy even more great meals later.

Besides checking that each recipe works perfectly in the slow cooker, our Test Kitchen registered dietitians make sure each recipe also delivers healthful amounts of calories, carbs, and sodium. Because they know you and I don't want to deprive ourselves, they recommend diabetes-friendly, satisfying serving sizes. And to help you tally your nutrient intake and follow your meal plan, you will find a nutrition analysis with each recipe.

Turn to this mouthwatering recipe collection to help you put diabetes on the back burner and move healthful, satisfying food to the front. Amaze yourself with what you really can eat—be sure to check out the collection of updated appetizers and desserts. Don't miss Mediterranean Beef Ragoût on page 71 and Chili Bean-Stuffed Peppers on page 66. These are a couple my family often requests. I'm sure your family will discover favorites, too.

Kelly Rawlings

Kelly Rawlings, PWD type 1
Editor, *Diabetic Living*® magazine

ON THE COVER:
Coq au Vin Stew
  (recipe, page 90).
Photographer: Scott Little.
Food stylist: Jennifer Petersen.

CONSUMER MARKETING

Vice President, Consumer Marketing	DAVID BALL
Consumer Product Marketing Director	STEVE SWANSON
Consumer Product Marketing Manager	WENDY MERICAL
Business Manager	TODD VOSS
Associate Director, Production	DOUGLAS M. JOHNSTON

Contributing Editorial Director	SHELLI MCCONNELL
Contributing Design Director	JILL BUDDEN
Contributing Copy Editor	GRETCHEN KAUFFMAN
Contributing Proofreader	CARRIE SCHMITZ
Test Kitchen Director	LYNN BLANCHARD
Test Kitchen Product Supervisor	LAURA MARZEN, R.D.
Editorial Assistants	LORI EGGERS, MARLENE TODD

DIABETIC LIVING® MAGAZINE

Editor in Chief	DEBORAH GORE OHRN
Executive Editor	BRIDGET SANDQUIST
Editor	KELLY RAWLINGS
Art Director	MICHELLE BILYEU
Design Director	TERESA LAURENZO

MEREDITH PUBLISHING GROUP

President JACK GRIFFIN

Executive Vice President ANDY SAREYAN

Vice President, Manufacturing BRUCE HESTON

President and Chief Executive Officer STEPHEN M. LACY

Chairman of the Board WILLIAM T. KERR

In Memoriam — E.T. MEREDITH III (1933-2003)

Diabetic Living® *Favorite Slow Cooker Recipes* is part of a series published by Meredith Corp., 1716 Locust St., Des Moines, IA 50309-3023.

If you have comments or questions about the editorial material in *Diabetic Living*® *Favorite Slow Cooker Recipes*, write to the editor of *Diabetic Living*® magazine, Meredith Corp., 1716 Locust St., Des Moines, IA 50309-3023. Send an e-mail to diabeticliving@meredith.com or call 800/678-2651. *Diabetic Living*® magazine is available by subscription or on the newsstand. To order a subscription to *Diabetic Living*® magazine, go to *DiabeticLivingOnline.com*.

contents

HOW DOES IT WORK?

- Slow cookers have electric coils in the base or around the side that transmit heat to the insert. Low-heat settings are about 200°F, and high-heat settings are about 300°F.

- Even on the low-heat setting, properly functioning slow cookers will keep foods above the "danger zone" of 40°F to 140°F in which bacteria grow fastest.

- Slow, covered cooking imitates the time-honored technique of braising, in which meats, poultry, and vegetables are tightly covered in an oven or on the stove top.

- Slow-cooking times don't need to be precise; the cooking method is very forgiving. Being off by 30 or even 60 minutes won't adversely affect the final products.

The Golden Rules

1. **Fill the cooker** at least half full and no more than two-thirds full.

2. **Brown meat** before adding it to the slow cooker to add flavor and color.

3. **Trim excess fat** from meat and poultry before cooking. Skim fat from the cooking liquid or sauce before serving.

4. **Always thaw** frozen meat and poultry before cooking.

5. **Don't peek (keep a lid on it).** Every time you open the lid, you release valuable moisture and add 30 minutes to the cooking time.

6. **Allow your meals to cook** as long as needed.

slow cooker

Valuable info to know when using your

When buying a slow cooker look for...

✳ **A snug-fitting, see-through lid.**

✳ **A removable ceramic or stainless-steel insert or liner.** It's easier to clean if you can take it out of the cooker. The insert should also have large, sturdy handles to make it easier (and safer) to remove from the base. A stove-top-safe insert is an excellent feature for one-pan browning. Consider a stainless-steel insert if a ceramic insert feels too heavy.

✳ **A programmable timer to set the cooker to start if you will be gone all day.** (Note: The cooker should be set to start within 2 hours of filling it.) Some timers can be programmed to cook on high for a set time and automatically switch to low.

✳ **A timer that automatically shifts to keep-warm mode as soon as the timed cooking ends.** (Note: The cookers should not keep food on keep-warm mode for more than 2 hours.)

✳ **A cooker with wraparound heating elements, which may heat more evenly than a cooker with the element on the bottom.**

Hot steam will gather on the inside of the lid. To avoid burns, lift the lid gently and straight up without tilting until it's clear of the cooker.

Cut down on preparation time by using precut and frozen vegetables, canned tomatoes and soups, and seasoning blends.

Meat and poultry cook faster than vegetables, so cut vegetables into uniform pieces and place them close to the heat, either around the side of the slow cooker or at the bottom under the meat or poultry and liquid.

Dairy products break down during long cooking. Add any milk, cream, sour cream, or cream cheese during the last 15 to 30 minutes of cooking. Evaporated milk does not curdle, however, and can often be used as a substitute.

High altitudes require you to add about 30 extra minutes for each hour of cooking time called for in a slow-cooking recipe.

An oval-shape cooker is better suited to large, oblong cuts of meat and is easier to pour from than a round cooker.

snippets
handy countertop appliance.

Q What's the best invention since the cooker itself?

A Nylon slow cooker liners— these durable bags designed to fit inside the ceramic liner make cleanup a breeze. The liner and leftover cooking liquids in it should be left in the slow cooker insert until they cool to a safe temperature.

come clean

Before washing your slow cooker, let the ceramic liner cool to room temperature so it doesn't crack when put in the water. If the liner is removable, the dishwasher is a good option. If it's permanently attached to the base, clean it with a soft cloth and soapy warm water. Don't use abrasive cleaners or pads; they can damage the surface. If food sticks to the cooker, fill the liner with warm water; let it stand before you wash it.

classic
comfort foods

Cacciatore-Style Chicken

The modern slow cooker combines two age-old styles of cooking—braising and stewing. It's no wonder you can use it to successfully prepare so many classic recipes. Here you'll find a host of timeless favorites adapted for your slow cooker and created with your health in mind.

Cacciatore-Style Chicken

Serve this meal-in-a-pot chicken dish over a little pasta to mop up the delicious sauce.

SERVINGS 6 (2 drumsticks, about 1 cup sauce, and ½ cup pasta each)

CARB. PER SERVING 35 g

  2 cups fresh button mushrooms, halved or quartered
  2 medium onions, cut into wedges
  2 stalks celery, sliced (1 cup)
  2 medium carrots, chopped (1 cup)
  4 cloves garlic, minced
  3 tablespoons quick-cooking tapioca, crushed
  1 teaspoon dried oregano, crushed
  ¼ teaspoon salt
  ¼ teaspoon black pepper
  2 bay leaves
 12 chicken drumsticks (about 3 pounds), skinned
  ½ cup reduced-sodium chicken broth
  ¼ cup dry white wine or reduced-sodium chicken broth
  1 14.5-ounce can diced tomatoes, undrained
  1 medium yellow or red sweet pepper, cut into strips
  ⅓ cup tomato paste
  2 cups hot cooked spaghetti
  ¼ cup shredded fresh basil

1. In a 5- to 6-quart slow cooker, combine mushrooms, onions, celery, carrots, and garlic. Sprinkle with tapioca, oregano, salt, black pepper, and bay leaves. Add chicken. Pour broth and wine over all in cooker.

2. Cover and cook on low-heat setting for 7 to 8 hours or on high-heat setting for 3½ to 4 hours.

3. If using low-heat setting, turn to high-heat setting. Stir in undrained tomatoes, sweet pepper, and tomato paste. Cover and cook for 15 minutes more. Discard bay leaves.

4. Serve chicken and tomato mixture over hot cooked spaghetti. Top with fresh basil.

PER SERVING: 324 cal., 5 g total fat (1 g sat. fat), 98 mg chol., 408 mg sodium, 35 g carb., 4 g fiber, 33 g pro. Exchanges: 2 vegetable, 1.5 starch, 3.5 lean meat. Carb choices: 2.

Chicken and Vegetables with Herbs

Frozen whole small onions are a nifty way to add lots of onion flavor to dishes of all kinds. There's no need to blanch and peel them, as you would fresh pearl onions.

SERVINGS 4 (2 chicken pieces, scant ½ cup vegetable mixture, and scant ½ cup sauce each)

CARB. PER SERVING 10 g

    8 ounces fresh button mushrooms, halved
 1½ cups frozen small whole onions
    ½ cup reduced-sodium chicken broth
    ¼ cup dry red wine or reduced-sodium chicken broth
    2 tablespoons tomato paste
    ½ teaspoon garlic salt
    ½ teaspoon dried rosemary, crushed
    ½ teaspoon dried thyme, crushed
    ¼ teaspoon black pepper
    1 bay leaf
    8 small chicken thighs and/or drumsticks (about 2 pounds), skinned
      Reduced-sodium chicken broth
    ¼ cup reduced-sodium chicken broth
    2 tablespoons all-purpose flour
      Baby lettuce (optional)

1. In a 4- to 5-quart slow cooker, combine mushrooms and whole onions. Stir in ½ cup broth, the wine, tomato paste, garlic salt, rosemary, thyme, pepper, and bay leaf. Add chicken.

2. Cover and cook on low-heat setting for 7 hours or on high-heat setting for 3½ hours.

3. Using a slotted spoon, transfer chicken and vegetables to a serving platter. Discard bay leaf. Cover chicken and vegetables to keep warm.

4. For sauce, skim fat from cooking liquid. Measure 1¾ cups of the cooking liquid, adding additional chicken broth, if necessary, to equal 1¾ cups total liquid. Transfer liquid to a medium saucepan. In a small bowl, combine ¼ cup broth and the flour until smooth; stir into liquid in saucepan. Cook and stir until thickened and bubbly; cook and stir for 1 minute more. Spoon some of the sauce over chicken. Pass remaining sauce. If desired, serve with baby lettuce.

PER SERVING: 215 cal., 5 g total fat (1 g sat. fat), 107 mg chol., 342 mg sodium, 10 g carb., 2 g fiber, 29 g pro. Exchanges: 1.5 vegetable, 3.5 lean meat, 0.5 fat. Carb choices: 0.5.

Country Captain

The golden-red sauce and fragrant spice blend bring taste buds to attention even before the first bite of tender chicken. Don't skip the currants; their fruity sweetness accents the curry flavor.

SERVINGS 6

CARB. PER SERVING 32 g

    1 medium sweet onion, cut into thin wedges
    3 pounds chicken drumsticks and/or thighs, skinned
    1 medium green sweet pepper, cut into thin strips
    1 medium yellow sweet pepper, cut into thin strips
    ¼ cup currants or golden raisins
    2 cloves garlic, minced
    1 14.5-ounce can diced tomatoes, undrained
    2 tablespoons quick-cooking tapioca, crushed
    2 to 3 teaspoons curry powder
    ½ teaspoon salt
    ½ teaspoon ground cumin
    ¼ teaspoon ground mace
    2 cups hot cooked white or brown rice
    2 tablespoons chopped green onion
    2 tablespoons sliced almonds, toasted

1. In a 3½- or 4-quart slow cooker, place onion, chicken, sweet peppers, currants, and garlic. In a large bowl, combine undrained tomatoes, tapioca, curry powder, salt, cumin, and mace. Pour over all in cooker.

2. Cover and cook on low-heat setting for 5 to 6 hours or on high-heat setting for 2½ to 3 hours.

3. Serve chicken mixture over hot cooked rice. Sprinkle with green onion and almonds.

PER SERVING: 298 cal., 6 g total fat (1 g sat. fat), 98 mg chol., 619 mg sodium, 32 g carb., 3 g fiber, 30 g pro. Exchanges: 1 vegetable, 1.5 starch, 3.5 lean meat. Carb choices: 2.

If your daily meal plan has some carbs to spare, serve this gravylike sauce and chicken with a spoonful of creamy mashed potatoes or cooked egg noodles.

Chicken and Vegetables with Herbs

Chicken Osso Buco

Although osso buco usually features veal shanks, chicken drumsticks make a tasty substitute.

SERVINGS 6 (2 drumsticks, 2/3 cup sauce, and 1/2 cup pasta each)

CARB. PER SERVING 33 g

- 2 tablespoons all-purpose flour
- 1/2 teaspoon salt
- 1/4 teaspoon black pepper
- 12 medium chicken drumsticks (about 3 pounds), skinned
- 1 tablespoon olive oil
- 2 medium carrots, chopped (1 cup)
- 1 large onion, chopped (1 cup)
- 2 stalks celery, chopped (1 cup)
- 6 cloves garlic, minced
- 2 tablespoons quick-cooking tapioca
- 1 8-ounce can tomato sauce
- 1/2 cup dry white wine or reduced-sodium chicken broth
- 1/4 cup reduced-sodium chicken broth
- 1 teaspoon finely shredded lemon peel
- 1 tablespoon lemon juice
- 1 teaspoon dried thyme, crushed
- 3 cups hot cooked multigrain penne pasta
  Snipped fresh parsley (optional)

1. Place flour, salt, and pepper in a resealable plastic bag. Add chicken, a few pieces at time, shaking to coat. In a 10-inch skillet, brown chicken, half at a time, in hot oil over medium heat about 10 minutes, turning once. Set aside.

2. In a 4- to 5-quart slow cooker, combine carrots, onion, celery, and garlic. Sprinkle with tapioca. Place chicken on top of vegetables. In a medium bowl, stir together tomato sauce, wine, broth, lemon peel, lemon juice, and thyme; pour over chicken in cooker.

3. Cover and cook on low-heat setting for 5 to 6 hours or on high-heat setting for 2 1/2 to 3 hours.

4. Serve chicken and sauce over hot cooked pasta. If desired, garnish with snipped parsley.

PER SERVING: 345 cal., 7 g total fat (1 g sat. fat), 98 mg chol., 522 mg sodium, 33 g carb., 4 g fiber, 33 g pro. Exchanges: 1 vegetable, 1.5 starch, 4 lean meat, 0.5 fat. Carb choices: 2.

Chicken Merlot with Mushrooms

Expect the sauce to be amber color if you opt to use chicken broth instead of the ruby Merlot.

SERVINGS 6

CARB. PER SERVING 12 g

- 3 cups sliced fresh button mushrooms (8 ounces)
- 1 large onion, chopped (1 cup)
- 2 cloves garlic, minced
- 2 1/2 to 3 pounds meaty chicken pieces (breast halves, thighs, and drumsticks), skinned
- 3/4 cup reduced-sodium chicken broth
- 1 6-ounce can tomato paste
- 1/4 cup Merlot or other dry red wine or reduced-sodium chicken broth
- 1 1/2 teaspoons dried basil, crushed
- 1/4 teaspoon salt
- 1/4 teaspoon black pepper
- 2 tablespoons cornstarch
- 2 tablespoons cold water
- 3 tablespoons shredded Parmesan cheese

1. In a 3 1/2- to 5-quart slow cooker, place mushrooms, onion, and garlic. Place chicken on top of vegetables. In a medium bowl, combine broth, tomato paste, wine, basil, salt, and pepper; pour over all in cooker.

2. Cover and cook on low-heat setting for 5 to 6 hours or on high-heat setting for 2 1/2 to 3 hours.

3. Transfer chicken and vegetables to a serving platter, reserving liquid in cooker. Cover chicken and vegetables to keep warm.

4. If using low-heat setting, turn to high-heat setting. In a small bowl, combine cornstarch and the water. Stir into liquid in cooker. Cover and cook about 15 minutes more or until thickened. Spoon sauce over chicken. Sprinkle individual servings with Parmesan cheese.

PER SERVING: 210 cal., 3 g total fat (1 g sat. fat), 80 mg chol., 301 mg sodium, 12 g carb., 2 g fiber, 30 g pro. Exchanges: 1.5 vegetable, 4 lean meat. Carb choices: 1.

Home-Style Chicken
and Noodles

Home-Style Chicken and Noodles

*If using fresh onions, cook in enough boiling water
to cover for 30 to 60 seconds; drain and rinse with
cold water. Cut off root ends and slip off peels.*

SERVINGS 8 (1¼ cups each)

CARB. PER SERVING 35 g

- 3 medium carrots, peeled and cut into 1-inch pieces
- 2 medium parsnips, peeled and cut into 1-inch pieces
- 1 cup pearl onions or frozen small whole onions
- 2 stalks celery, cut into 1-inch pieces
- 3 whole chicken legs (drumsticks and thighs) (about 3 pounds), skinned
- ½ teaspoon dried thyme, crushed
- ½ teaspoon dried sage, crushed
- 2 cloves garlic, minced
- ½ teaspoon salt
- ¼ teaspoon black pepper
- 2 14-ounce cans reduced-sodium chicken broth
- ¼ cup dry sherry or reduced-sodium chicken broth
- 1 12-ounce package frozen egg noodles
- ¾ cup frozen peas
- 4 or 5 fresh sage leaves (optional)

1. In a 5- to 6-quart slow cooker, place carrots, parsnips, onions, and celery. Top with chicken; sprinkle with thyme, sage, garlic, salt, and pepper. Pour chicken broth and sherry over all in cooker.

2. Cover and cook on low-heat setting for 7 hours or on high-heat setting for 3 hours. Stir in noodles. If using low-heat setting, turn to high-heat setting. Cover and cook for 1 to 1½ hours more or until noodles are tender.

3. Remove chicken. When cool enough to handle, remove meat from bones. Coarsely shred chicken and stir into mixture in cooker. Add peas; cover and let stand for 5 minutes. If desired, garnish with fresh sage.

PER SERVING: 301 cal., 5 g total fat (1 g sat. fat), 127 mg chol., 497 mg sodium, 35 g carb., 4 g fiber, 26 g pro. Exchanges: 0.5 vegetable, 2 starch, 3 lean meat. Carb choices: 2.

Smokin' Jambalaya

Smoked turkey sausage comes packaged as a piece larger than this Southern-style dish calls for. Wrap the leftover portion in freezer wrap and freeze for another use.

SERVINGS 6

CARB. PER SERVING 28 g

1½ pounds skinless, boneless chicken thighs
4 ounces smoked turkey sausage
1 large onion, chopped (1 cup)
2 stalks celery, thinly sliced (1 cup)
1 14.5-ounce can fire-roasted diced tomatoes, undrained
1 cup reduced-sodium chicken broth
2 tablespoons tomato paste
2 tablespoons quick-cooking tapioca, crushed
1 tablespoon Worcestershire sauce
1 tablespoon lemon juice
1 fresh serrano chile pepper, seeded and finely chopped*
3 cloves garlic, minced
½ teaspoon dried thyme, crushed
½ teaspoon dried oregano, crushed
¼ teaspoon cayenne pepper
⅛ teaspoon salt
8 ounces medium shrimp, peeled and deveined
½ cup chopped yellow sweet pepper
2 cups frozen cut okra
1 14.8-ounce pouch cooked long grain or brown rice

1. Cut chicken and sausage into bite-size pieces. In a 3½- or 4-quart slow cooker, combine chicken, sausage, onion, and celery. Stir in undrained tomatoes, broth, tomato paste, tapioca, Worcestershire sauce, lemon juice, serrano pepper, garlic, thyme, oregano, cayenne pepper, and salt.

2. Cover and cook on low-heat setting for 6 to 8 hours or on high-heat setting for 3 to 4 hours.

3. If using low-heat setting, turn to high-heat setting. Stir in shrimp, sweet pepper, and okra. Cover and cook about 30 minutes more or until shrimp turn opaque.

4. Prepare rice according to package directions; serve with jambalaya.

*TEST KITCHEN TIP: Because hot chile peppers contain volatile oils that can burn your skin and eyes, avoid direct contact with chiles as much as possible. When working with chiles, wear plastic or rubber gloves. If your bare hands do touch the chiles, wash your hands well with soap and water.

PER SERVING: 276 cal., 6 g total fat (1 g sat. fat), 112 mg chol., 490 mg sodium, 28 g carb., 3 g fiber, 26 g pro. Exchanges: 1 vegetable, 1.5 starch, 3 lean meat. Carb choices: 2.

Smokin' Jambalaya

Turkey and Dumplings

If your family prefers chicken over turkey, substitute skinless, boneless chicken breast halves for the turkey breast tenderloins.

SERVINGS 6

CARB. PER SERVING 32 g

3 medium carrots, thinly sliced (1½ cups)
3 stalks celery, thinly sliced (1½ cups)
1 medium onion, cut into very thin wedges
1¼ pounds turkey breast tenderloins, cut into ¾-inch cubes
1 14-ounce can reduced-sodium chicken broth
1 10.75-ounce can reduced-fat and reduced-sodium condensed cream of chicken soup
2 teaspoons dried leaf sage, crushed
¼ teaspoon black pepper

Rosemary Turkey with Vegetables

1 cup all-purpose flour
1 teaspoon baking powder
⅛ teaspoon salt
2 tablespoons shortening
½ cup fat-free milk
¼ cup all-purpose flour

1. In a 3½- or 4-quart slow cooker, combine carrots, celery, and onion; stir in turkey. Set aside ½ cup of the broth. In a medium bowl, combine remaining broth, the soup, sage, and pepper; stir into mixture in cooker.
2. Cover and cook on low-heat setting for 6 to 7 hours or on high-heat setting for 3 to 3½ hours.
3. For dumplings, stir together the 1 cup flour, the baking powder, and salt. Using a pastry blender, cut in shortening until mixture resembles coarse crumbs. Add milk and stir just until moistened.
4. If using low-heat setting, turn to high-heat setting. In a small bowl, whisk together reserved ½ cup broth and the ¼ cup flour; stir into mixture in cooker. Drop dumpling dough by small spoonfuls on top of mixture in cooker. Cover and cook for 45 minutes more.
5. Remove liner from slow cooker, if possible, or turn off slow cooker. Let stand, covered, for 15 minutes before serving.
PER SERVING: 300 cal., 6 g total fat (2 g sat. fat), 63 mg chol., 516 mg sodium, 32 g carb., 3 g fiber, 29 g pro. Exchanges: 0.5 vegetable, 2 starch, 3 lean meat. Carb choices: 2.

Rosemary Turkey with Vegetables

Why make turkey and all the trimmings a holiday-only treat? A turkey breast half is a manageable cut to use for everyday cooking in your slow cooker.
SERVINGS 8 (about 3½ ounces turkey with vegetables and scant ¼ cup gravy each)
CARB. PER SERVING 23 g

1 teaspoon dried rosemary, crushed
¼ teaspoon salt
¼ teaspoon garlic powder
¼ teaspoon dried thyme, crushed
¼ teaspoon black pepper
1 2¾- to 3¼-pound turkey breast half with bone, skinned
1 tablespoon cooking oil
Nonstick cooking spray
1¼ pounds new potatoes, halved
8 medium carrots, peeled and cut into 2- to 3-inch-long pieces
1 large onion, cut into ½-inch wedges
¼ cup reduced-sodium chicken broth
Reduced-sodium chicken broth
¼ cup all-purpose flour

1. In a small bowl, combine rosemary, salt, garlic powder, thyme, and pepper. Rub over turkey breast. In a very large skillet, brown turkey breast on all sides in hot oil over medium heat. Lightly coat the inside of a 5- to 6-quart slow cooker with cooking spray. In prepared cooker, place potatoes, carrots, onion, and the ¼ cup broth. Top with turkey.
2. Cover and cook on low-heat setting for 9 hours or on high-heat setting for 4½ hours.
3. Transfer turkey to a cutting board. Cover turkey loosely with foil and let stand for 15 minutes. Meanwhile, using a slotted spoon, transfer vegetables to a serving platter; keep warm.
4. For gravy, strain cooking liquid into a 2-cup measure. Add enough chicken broth to equal 1¾ cups. In a medium saucepan, whisk together broth mixture and flour. Cook and stir over medium heat until thickened and bubbly; cook and stir for 1 minute more. Season to taste with additional pepper.
5. Cut turkey meat off the bone. Slice turkey and serve with vegetables and gravy.
PER SERVING: 256 cal., 3 g total fat (0 g sat. fat), 76 mg chol., 272 mg sodium, 23 g carb., 4 g fiber, 34 g pro. Exchanges: 0.5 vegetable, 1 starch, 4 lean meat. Carb choices: 1.5.

Turkey and Pasta
Primavera

Classic Beef Stroganoff

*Beef Stroganoff usually features tenderloin or sirloin steak.
This recipe calls for stew meat, which is more economical
and lets the slow cooker work its simmering magic
for rich and tender results.*

SERVINGS 6 (about ¾ cup each)

CARB. PER SERVING 8 g

1½ pounds beef stew meat
1 tablespoon cooking oil
2 cups sliced fresh button mushrooms
½ cup sliced green onions (4) or chopped onion
    (1 medium)
2 cloves garlic, minced
½ teaspoon dried oregano, crushed
½ teaspoon salt
¼ teaspoon dried thyme, crushed
¼ teaspoon black pepper
1 bay leaf
1½ cups lower-sodium beef broth
⅓ cup dry sherry
1 8-ounce carton light sour cream
¼ cup cold water
2 tablespoons cornstarch
    Snipped fresh parsley (optional)

1. Trim fat from meat. Cut meat into 1-inch pieces.
In a large skillet, cook meat, half at a time, in hot oil
over medium heat until browned. Drain off fat. Set
aside meat.
2. In a 3½- or 4-quart slow cooker, place mushrooms,
onions, garlic, oregano, salt, thyme, pepper, and bay
leaf. Add meat. Pour broth and sherry over all in cooker.
3. Cover and cook on low-heat setting for 8 to 10 hours
or on high-heat setting for 4 to 5 hours. Discard bay leaf.
4. If using low-heat setting, turn to high-heat setting.
In a medium bowl, combine sour cream, the water,
and cornstarch. Stir about 1 cup of the hot cooking
liquid into sour cream mixture. Stir sour cream mixture
into cooker. Cover and cook about 30 minutes more
or until thickened. If desired, sprinkle each serving
with parsley.
PER SERVING: 248 cal., 9 g total fat (4 g sat. fat), 79 mg chol.,
408 mg sodium, 8 g carb., 1 g fiber, 28 g pro. Exchanges:
1 vegetable, 4 lean meat. Carb choices: 0.5.

Turkey and Pasta Primavera

*A sprinkling of Parmesan cheese brings
a tantalizingly sharp note to this creamy blend of
turkey, pasta, and vegetables.*

SERVINGS 6 (about 1¼ cups each)

CARB. PER SERVING 36 g

1½ pounds turkey breast tenderloins or skinless, boneless
    chicken breast halves, cut into 1-inch pieces
1 16-ounce package frozen stir-fry vegetables (sugar
    snap peas, carrots, onions, and mushrooms)
1½ teaspoons dried basil, oregano, or Italian seasoning,
    crushed
1 10-ounce carton refrigerated light Alfredo pasta sauce
8 ounces dried linguine or spaghetti, broken
¼ cup shredded Parmesan cheese (1 ounce)

1. In a 3½- to 5-quart slow cooker, combine turkey
pieces and frozen vegetables. Sprinkle with basil. Stir in
Alfredo sauce.
2. Cover and cook on low-heat setting for 4 hours or on
high-heat setting for 2 hours.
3. Cook pasta according to package directions; drain.
Stir pasta into mixture in slow cooker. Sprinkle
individual servings with Parmesan cheese.
PER SERVING: 373 cal., 7 g total fat (4 g sat. fat), 84 mg chol.,
394 mg sodium, 36 g carb., 2 g fiber, 38 g pro. Exchanges:
1 vegetable, 2 starch, 4 lean meat. Carb choices: 2.5.

Bloody Mary Steak

Sassy and lively—just like the classic cocktail—this easy-fixing steak is sensational.

SERVINGS 6

CARB. PER SERVING 3 g

1 2-pound beef round steak, cut ¾ inch thick
Nonstick cooking spray
¾ cup hot-style tomato juice
2 cloves garlic, minced
¼ cup water
4 teaspoons cornstarch
2 tablespoons cold water
2 teaspoons prepared horseradish

1. Trim fat from steak. Cut steak into six serving-size pieces. Lightly coat an unheated large skillet with cooking spray; heat skillet over medium-high heat. Add steak pieces; cook until browned, turning once. Place steak in a 2½- to 3½-quart slow cooker. Add tomato juice, garlic, and the ¼ cup water.
2. Cover and cook on low-heat setting for 8 to 9 hours or on high-heat setting for 4 to 4½ hours.
3. Transfer steak to a serving platter, reserving cooking liquid. If desired, slice steak; cover to keep warm.
4. For gravy, pour cooking liquid into a glass measuring cup; skim off fat. Measure liquid; add water if necessary to reach 1½ cups liquid. In a small saucepan, combine cornstarch and the 2 tablespoons cold water; stir in cooking liquid. Cook and stir over medium heat until thickened and bubbly; cook and stir for 2 minutes more. Stir in horseradish. Serve steak with gravy.

PER SERVING: 208 cal., 7 g total fat (2 g sat. fat), 88 mg chol., 177 mg sodium, 3 g carb., 0 g fiber, 34 g pro. Exchanges: 4.5 lean meat. Carb choices: 0.

Bloody Mary Steak

Piquant Pot Roast

Just 1 teaspoon of horseradish gives this succulent pot roast a hint of zesty flavor. For more zing, use 2 teaspoons.

SERVINGS 8 (3 ounces meat and about 3 tablespoons sauce each)

CARB. PER SERVING 5 g

1 2- to 2½-pound boneless beef chuck pot roast
2 medium onions, cut into wedges
1 8-ounce can tomato sauce
¼ cup water
1 tablespoon yellow mustard
1 to 2 teaspoons prepared horseradish
½ teaspoon salt
¼ teaspoon black pepper
2 tablespoons all-purpose flour
2 tablespoons cold water

1. Trim fat from roast. If necessary, cut roast to fit in a 3½- or 4-quart slow cooker. Place roast in the cooker. Top with onions. In a small bowl, combine tomato sauce, the ¼ cup water, the mustard, horseradish, salt, and pepper; pour over all in cooker.
2. Cover and cook on low-heat setting for 8 to 10 hours or on high-heat setting for 4 to 5 hours.
3. Transfer roast and onions to a serving platter; cover to keep warm. For sauce, transfer cooking liquid to a small saucepan. Skim off fat. In a small bowl, stir together flour and the 2 tablespoons cold water. Stir into mixture in saucepan. Cook and stir over medium heat until thickened and bubbly; cook and stir for 1 minute more. Serve with roast and onions.

PER SERVING: 171 cal., 5 g total fat (2 g sat. fat), 67 mg chol., 375 mg sodium, 5 g carb., 1 g fiber, 25 g pro. Exchanges: 0.5 vegetable, 3.5 very lean meat, 1 fat. Carb choices: 0.

Saucy Pot Roast with Noodles

For a complete meal, team this old-fashioned family-gathering favorite with a tossed salad.
SERVINGS 8 (3 ounces meat, 1/3 cup vegetable mixture, and 1/2 cup noodles each)
CARB. PER SERVING 35 g

1 2- to 2 1/2-pound boneless beef chuck pot roast
Nonstick cooking spray
2 medium carrots, sliced (1 cup)
2 stalks celery, sliced (1 cup)
1 medium onion, sliced
2 cloves garlic, minced
1 tablespoon quick-cooking tapioca
1 14.5-ounce can Italian-style stewed tomatoes, undrained
1 6-ounce can Italian-style tomato paste
1/4 teaspoon black pepper
1 bay leaf
4 cups hot cooked noodles

1. Trim fat from roast. If necessary, cut roast to fit in a 3 1/2- or 4-quart slow cooker. Coat a large nonstick skillet with cooking spray; heat skillet over medium heat. Brown roast on all sides in hot skillet.
2. In the cooker, combine carrots, celery, onion, and garlic. Sprinkle tapioca over vegetables. Place roast on top of vegetables.
3. In a medium bowl, combine undrained tomatoes, tomato paste, pepper, and bay leaf; pour over all in cooker.
4. Cover and cook on low-heat setting for 8 to 10 hours or on high-setting for 4 to 5 hours.
5. Discard bay leaf. Cut meat into serving-size portions. Serve with hot cooked noodles. If desired, garnish with *celery leaves.*
PER SERVING: 324 cal., 7 g total fat (2 g sat. fat), 73 mg chol., 586 mg sodium, 35 g carb., 3 g fiber, 31 g pro. Exchanges: 1 vegetable, 2 starch, 3 lean meat. Carb choices: 2.

Saucy Pot Roast with Noodles

Cowboy Beef

Pot roast heads for the untamed West when slow-cooked with chili beans, corn, tomatoes, and spicy chile peppers in adobo sauce.
SERVINGS 8
CARB. PER SERVING 14 g

1 2- to 2 1/2-pound boneless beef chuck pot roast
1 15-ounce can chili beans with chili gravy
1 11-ounce can whole kernel corn with sweet peppers, drained
1 10-ounce can chopped tomatoes and green chile peppers, undrained
1 to 2 teaspoons finely chopped canned chipotle chile peppers in adobo sauce

1. Trim fat from roast. If necessary, cut roast to fit in a 3 1/2- or 4-quart slow cooker. Place roast in the cooker. In a medium bowl, stir together the undrained beans, drained corn, undrained tomatoes, and the chipotle peppers. Pour bean mixture over roast in cooker.
2. Cover and cook on low-heat setting for 10 to 12 hours or on high-heat setting for 5 to 6 hours.
3. Transfer roast to a cutting board. Pull meat into pieces and arrange in a shallow serving bowl. Using a slotted spoon, spoon bean mixture into bowl with meat. Drizzle some of the cooking liquid over roast and bean mixture to moisten.
PER SERVING: 223 cal., 5 g total fat (2 g sat. fat), 50 mg chol., 473 mg sodium, 14 g carb., 4 g fiber, 29 g pro. Exchanges: 1 starch, 3.5 lean meat. Carb choices: 1.

Cowboy Beef

Beef Burgundy

Turkey bacon provides the same crunch and yummy flavor as traditional bacon, but it is lower in fat.

SERVINGS 8

CARB. PER SERVING 27 g

- 3 slices turkey bacon, coarsely chopped
- 2 pounds boneless beef chuck pot roast, cut into 1-inch pieces
- 2 teaspoons olive oil
- 1½ cups chopped onions
- 2 cloves garlic, minced
- 4 stems fresh Italian (flat-leaf) parsley
- 3 sprigs fresh thyme
- 1 sprig fresh rosemary
- 2 bay leaves
- ¼ teaspoon whole black peppercorns
- 4 medium carrots, cut into ¾-inch pieces
- 2 cups frozen small whole onions
- 3 tablespoons quick-cooking tapioca, crushed
- 1 cup Burgundy wine or lower-sodium beef broth
- ½ cup lower-sodium beef broth
- ¼ cup brandy or lower-sodium beef broth
- 1 tablespoon tomato paste
- 1 cup quartered fresh cremini mushrooms
- 2 teaspoons olive oil

Skins-On Garlic Mashed Potatoes (page 21)

Chopped fresh Italian (flat-leaf) parsley

Beef Burgundy

1. In a large nonstick skillet, cook bacon until cooked through. Remove from skillet; drain on paper towels. Cover and chill cooked bacon until serving time. In the same skillet, brown half of the beef in 2 teaspoons hot oil over medium heat; remove from skillet. Add remaining beef, chopped onions, and garlic to skillet; cook until meat is browned and onions are tender. Remove from heat; combine all meat in skillet.

2. For the bouquet garni, place parsley stems, thyme sprigs, rosemary sprig, bay leaves, and peppercorns in the center of an 8-inch square of 100-percent-cotton cheesecloth. Gather corners together and tie with a piece of 100-percent-cotton kitchen string.

3. Place carrots and small whole onions in a 3½- or 4-quart slow cooker. Sprinkle with tapioca. Place meat mixture on top of vegetables. Add bouquet garni. Whisk together wine, broth, brandy, and tomato paste. Pour over all in cooker.

4. Cover and cook on low-heat setting for 10 to 12 hours or on high-heat setting for 5 to 6 hours. Discard the bouquet garni.

5. In a large skillet, cook mushrooms in 2 teaspoons hot oil over medium-high heat until browned. Serve beef mixture with mashed potatoes. Top each serving with bacon, mushrooms, and chopped parsley.

SKINS-ON GARLIC MASHED POTATOES: Cut 1⅓ pounds red-skin, Yukon gold, or russet potatoes into quarters. In a covered large saucepan, cook potatoes and 4 garlic cloves, peeled and halved, in enough boiling lightly salted water to cover for 20 to 25 minutes or until tender; drain. Mash with potato masher or beat with an electric mixer on low speed. Add 1 tablespoon butter, ⅛ teaspoon salt, and ⅛ teaspoon black pepper. Slowly beat in fat-free milk (3 to 5 tablespoons) until potato mixture is light and fluffy.

PER SERVING: 356 cal., 10 g total fat (3 g sat. fat), 59 mg chol., 289 mg sodium, 27 g carb., 4 g fiber, 30 g pro. Exchanges: 1 vegetable, 1.5 starch, 3.5 lean meat, 1 fat. Carb choices: 2.

Short Ribs with Leeks

Lemon peel brightens the flavor of this savory dish. It's perfect when you have a house full of guests—you'll be able to spend time with them instead of in the kitchen.

SERVINGS 6 (4 ounces meat, ⅔ cup vegetables, and about ¼ cup sauce each)
CARB. PER SERVING 16 g

8	ounces fresh button mushrooms, halved
4	medium carrots, cut into 1-inch pieces
4	medium leeks, trimmed and cut into 1-inch slices
2	pounds boneless beef short ribs
2	teaspoons finely shredded lemon peel
½	teaspoon black pepper
½	teaspoon dried rosemary, crushed
½	teaspoon dried thyme, crushed
½	teaspoon salt
¾	cup lower-sodium beef broth
⅓	cup light sour cream
4	teaspoons all-purpose flour

1. In a 3½- or 4-quart slow cooker, place mushrooms, carrots, and leeks. Place ribs on top of vegetables. Sprinkle with lemon peel, pepper, rosemary, thyme, and salt. Pour broth over all in cooker.

2. Cover and cook on low-heat setting for 7 to 8 hours or on high-heat setting for 3½ to 4 hours.

3. Using a slotted spoon, transfer meat and vegetables to a serving dish. Cover to keep warm. Skim fat from cooking liquid. Measure 1 cup cooking liquid. In a small saucepan, stir together sour cream and flour. Whisk in 1 cup cooking liquid. Cook and stir over medium heat until slightly thickened and bubbly; cook and stir for 1 minute more. Ladle sauce over meat and vegetables to serve.

PER SERVING: 318 cal., 14 g total fat (6 g sat. fat), 90 mg chol., 397 mg sodium, 16 g carb., 3 g fiber, 32 g pro. Exchanges: 1.5 vegetable, 0.5 carb., 3.5 lean meat, 2 fat. Carb choices: 1.

Short ribs, about 2×3 inches in size, are usually taken from the chuck cut, making them economical fare. These tough little cuts are naturals for braising in the slow cooker.

Tried-and-True Chili Mac

It's tempting to overindulge in this knock-your-socks-off meal in a bowl. Control your craving by measuring your portion before you dig in.

Tried-and-True Chili Mac

Corkscrew-shape cavatappi is fun in this beloved kid favorite, but elbow macaroni works just as well.

SERVINGS 8 (about 1 cup each)

CARB. PER SERVING 36 g

- 1½ pounds lean ground beef
- 1 large onion, chopped (1 cup)
- 3 cloves garlic, minced
- 1 15-ounce can chili beans in chili gravy, undrained
- 1 14.5-ounce can diced tomatoes and green chiles, undrained
- 1 cup lower-sodium beef broth
- 1 medium green sweet pepper, chopped (¾ cup)
- 2 teaspoons chili powder
- 1 teaspoon ground cumin
- 8 ounces dried cavatappi or elbow macaroni, cooked according to package directions
- ¼ cup shredded reduced-fat cheddar cheese (1 ounce)

1. In a skillet, cook beef, onion, and garlic until meat is browned and onion is tender. Drain off fat.

2. In a 3½- or 4-quart slow cooker, combine meat mixture, undrained chili beans, undrained tomatoes, broth, sweet pepper, chili powder, and cumin.

3. Cover and cook on low-heat setting for 4 to 6 hours or on high-heat setting for 2 to 3 hours. Just before serving, stir in cooked pasta. Top each serving with cheese.

PER SERVING: 343 cal., 10 g total fat (4 g sat. fat), 58 mg chol., 510 mg sodium, 36 g carb., 5 g fiber, 26 g pro. Exchanges: 0.5 vegetable, 2 starch, 2.5 medium-fat meat. Carb choices: 2.5.

Mediterranean Meat Loaf

Feta cheese, oregano, and dried tomatoes load this meat loaf with Mediterranean flavor.

SERVINGS 6

CARB. PER SERVING 10 g

- ¼ cup refrigerated or frozen egg product, thawed, or 1 egg, lightly beaten
- 2 tablespoons fat-free milk
- ½ cup fine dry bread crumbs
- ½ teaspoon salt
- ½ teaspoon dried oregano, crushed
- ¼ teaspoon black pepper
- 2 cloves garlic, minced
- 1½ pounds lean ground beef
- ½ cup crumbled reduced-fat feta cheese (2 ounces)
- ¼ cup oil-packed dried tomatoes, drained and snipped
- 3 tablespoons bottled pizza or pasta sauce

1. In a medium bowl, combine egg and milk; beat with a fork. Stir in bread crumbs, salt, oregano, pepper, and garlic. Add ground beef, feta cheese, and dried tomatoes; mix well. Shape meat mixture into a 5-inch round loaf.

2. Tear off an 18-inch-square piece of heavy foil. Cut into thirds. Fold each piece into thirds lengthwise. Crisscross strips and place meat loaf in center of foil strips. Bring up strips and transfer loaf and foil to a 3½- or 4-quart slow cooker (leave foil strips under loaf). Press loaf away from side of cooker. Fold down strips, leaving loaf exposed. Spread pizza sauce over loaf.

3. Cover and cook on low-heat setting for 7 to 8 hours or on high-heat setting for 3½ to 4 hours.

4. Using foil strips, carefully lift meat loaf from cooker. Discard foil strips.

PER SERVING: 282 cal., 14 g total fat (6 g sat. fat), 77 mg chol., 575 mg sodium, 10 g carb., 1 g fiber, 28 g pro. Exchanges: 0.5 starch, 3.5 medium-fat meat. Carb choices: 0.5.

Polenta with Ground Beef Ragoût

Sliced polenta on the bottom and a spoonful of pesto on top add a gourmet angle to this slow-simmered beef.

SERVINGS 6

CARB. PER SERVING 30 g

- 1 pound lean ground beef
- 1 14.5-ounce can Italian-style stewed tomatoes, undrained
- 3 medium carrots, cut into ½-inch-thick slices
- 2 medium onions, cut into thin wedges
- 1 large red sweet pepper, cut into 1-inch pieces
- ½ cup water
- ¼ teaspoon black pepper
- 6 cloves garlic, minced
- 1 medium zucchini, halved lengthwise and cut into ¼-inch-thick slices
- 1 16-ounce tube refrigerated cooked polenta
- ¼ cup purchased pesto
  Fresh basil sprigs (optional)

1. In a large skillet, cook ground beef until browned. Drain off fat. Transfer meat to a 3½- or 4-quart slow cooker. Stir in undrained tomatoes, carrots, onions, sweet pepper, the water, black pepper, and garlic.

2. Cover and cook on low-heat setting for 7 to 9 hours or on high-heat setting for 3½ to 4½ hours.

3. If using low-heat setting, turn to high-heat setting. Stir in zucchini. Cover and cook about 30 minutes more or until zucchini is crisp-tender.

4. Meanwhile, prepare polenta according to package directions. Serve meat mixture over polenta. Top individual servings with pesto. If desired, garnish with basil.

PER SERVING: 332 cal., 15 g total fat (3 g sat. fat), 51 mg chol., 677 mg sodium, 30 g carb., 5 g fiber, 20 g pro. Exchanges: 1.5 vegetable, 1.5 starch, 2 medium-fat meat, 0.5 fat. Carb choices: 2.

Herbed Apricot Pork Loin Roast

Italian Pork with
Mashed Sweet Potatoes

Relish a Roast

A stash of fork-tender cooked roast can come in handy for brown-bag lunches or quick dinners. Shred or cube any extra roast and try one of these clever ideas.

1. **Toss it** in a salad.
2. **Pile it** on an English muffin half for an open-face sandwich.
3. **Stuff it** in a whole wheat pita with an assortment of veggies.
4. **Stir some** into your favorite marinara sauce.
5. **Spice it up** with a little giardiniera mix.
6. **Roll it up** in a tortilla.
7. **Drizzle it** with a little barbecue sauce.
8. **Top a pizza** with it.
9. **Add a handful** to a side-dish salad to turn it into a main dish.
10. **Put some** in a pot of chili.

Italian Pork with Mashed Sweet Potatoes

A fennel seed rub coats this pork with extraordinary licoricelike flavor, and the golden-orange potatoes add just the right amount of sweetness.

SERVINGS 4 (3½ ounces meat and ½ cup potatoes each)
CARB. PER SERVING 24 g

- 1 teaspoon fennel seeds, crushed
- ½ teaspoon dried oregano, crushed
- ½ teaspoon garlic powder
- ½ teaspoon paprika
- ¼ teaspoon salt
- ¼ teaspoon black pepper
- 1 1½- to 2-pound boneless pork shoulder roast
- 1 pound sweet potatoes, peeled and cut into 1-inch pieces
- 1 cup reduced-sodium chicken broth

1. In a small bowl, combine fennel seeds, oregano, garlic powder, paprika, salt, and pepper. Trim fat from roast. Sprinkle fennel seed mixture evenly over roast; rub in with your fingers. If necessary, cut roast to fit in a 3½- or 4-quart slow cooker. Set aside roast.
2. Place sweet potatoes in cooker. Add roast. Pour broth over all in cooker.
3. Cover and cook on low-heat setting for 8 to 10 hours or on high-heat setting for 4 to 5 hours.
4. Remove meat from cooker, reserving cooking liquid. Slice meat. Using a slotted spoon, transfer sweet potatoes to a medium bowl. Use a potato masher to mash sweet potatoes, adding enough of the cooking liquid, if necessary, to moisten. Serve meat with mashed sweet potatoes.
PER SERVING: 341 cal., 10 g total fat (4 g sat. fat), 110 mg chol., 490 mg sodium, 24 g carb., 4 g fiber, 36 g pro. Exchanges: 1.5 starch, 4.5 lean meat, 0.5 fat. Carb choices: 1.5.

Herbed Apricot Pork Loin Roast

Treat your guests to a succulent pork roast draped with a golden herbed fruit sauce. The 15-minute standing time makes the tender meat easier to slice.

SERVINGS 8
CARB. PER SERVING 24 g

- 1 3-pound boneless pork top loin roast
- ¼ teaspoon salt
- ¼ teaspoon black pepper
- 1 10-ounce jar apricot spreadable fruit
- ⅓ cup finely chopped onion
- 2 tablespoons Dijon-style mustard
- 1 tablespoon brandy (optional)
- 1 teaspoon finely shredded lemon peel
- 1 teaspoon snipped fresh rosemary or ½ teaspoon dried rosemary, crushed
- 1 teaspoon snipped fresh sage or ½ teaspoon dried sage, crushed
- 1 teaspoon snipped fresh thyme or ½ teaspoon dried thyme, crushed
- ¼ teaspoon black pepper
- 2 tablespoons water
- 4 teaspoons cornstarch
- 4 fresh apricots, pitted and quartered
- Fresh thyme, sage, and/or rosemary (optional)

1. Season pork roast with salt and ¼ teaspoon pepper. In a medium bowl, combine spreadable fruit, onion, mustard, brandy (if using), lemon peel, rosemary, sage, thyme, and ¼ teaspoon pepper.
2. Place roast in a 4- to 5-quart slow cooker. Pour fruit mixture over roast.
3. Cover and cook on low-heat setting for 6 to 7 hours or on high-heat setting for 3 to 3½ hours.
4. Remove roast from cooker, reserving cooking liquid. Cover roast loosely with foil and let stand for 15 minutes before carving.
5. Meanwhile, in a medium saucepan, combine the water and cornstarch; carefully stir in liquid from cooker. Cook and stir sauce until thickened and bubbly; cook and stir for 2 minutes more. Serve sauce with pork and fresh apricots. If desired, garnish with fresh herbs.
PER SERVING: 322 cal., 7 g total fat (2 g sat. fat), 107 mg chol., 247 mg sodium, 24 g carb., 1 g fiber, 38 g pro. Exchanges: 1.5 carb., 5 lean meat. Carb choices: 1.5.

Home-Style Pork Pot Roast

Be sure to cut the vegetables in similar-size pieces so they cook to the same doneness.

SERVINGS 6

CARB. PER SERVING 29 g

- 1 2- to 2½-pound boneless pork shoulder roast
- 1 tablespoon cooking oil
- 3 tablespoons Dijon-style mustard
- 1 teaspoon dried thyme, crushed
- ½ teaspoon dried rosemary, crushed
- ¼ teaspoon black pepper
- 12 ounces round red potatoes, cut into 1-inch pieces
- 3 medium parsnips, cut into 1-inch pieces
- 3 medium carrots, cut into 1-inch pieces
- 1 large onion, cut into wedges
- ¾ cup canned seasoned chicken broth with roasted garlic
- 3 tablespoons quick-cooking tapioca

1. Trim fat from roast. If necessary, cut roast to fit in a 3½- or 4-quart slow cooker. In a large skillet, brown roast on all sides in hot oil. Brush roast with mustard. Sprinkle with thyme, rosemary, and pepper.

2. In the slow cooker, place potatoes, parsnips, carrots, and onion. Pour broth over vegetables. Sprinkle with tapioca. Place roast on top of vegetables.

3. Cover and cook on low-heat setting for 10 to 12 hours or on high-heat setting for 5 to 6 hours.

4. Transfer meat and vegetables to a serving platter. Strain cooking liquid; skim off fat. Drizzle some of the cooking liquid over meat; pass remaining liquid.

PER SERVING: 364 cal., 11 g total fat (3 g sat. fat), 98 mg chol., 453 mg sodium, 29 g carb., 5 g fiber, 33 g pro. Exchanges: 0.5 vegetable, 1.5 starch, 4 lean meat, 1 fat. Carb choices: 2.

Pork Ribs and Beans

When food lovers use terms like "rustic" and "country French," this dish is the type of simple, nourishing fare they have in mind.

SERVINGS 6 (4½ ounces meat and ⅔ cup bean mixture each)

CARB. PER SERVING 24 g

- 2 pounds boneless pork country-style ribs
- 1 teaspoon Italian seasoning, crushed
- ¾ teaspoon dried rosemary, crushed
- ¼ teaspoon black pepper
- 1 medium onion, chopped (½ cup)
- 1 15- or 19-ounce can white kidney (cannellini) beans, rinsed and drained
- 1 15-ounce can black beans, rinsed and drained
- 1 14.5-ounce can no-salt-added diced tomatoes, undrained
- ¼ cup dry red wine or water
- 3 tablespoons shredded Parmesan cheese (optional)

1. Trim fat from meat. Sprinkle meat with Italian seasoning, rosemary, and pepper. Place meat in a 3½- or 4-quart slow cooker. Place onion, beans, and undrained tomatoes on meat in cooker. Pour wine over all.

2. Cover and cook on low-heat setting for 8 to 9 hours or on high-heat setting for 4 to 4½ hours.

3. Using a slotted spoon, transfer meat and bean mixture to a serving platter. Spoon some of the cooking liquid over meat and beans. If desired, sprinkle individual servings with Parmesan cheese.

PER SERVING: 325 cal., 8 g total fat (3 g sat. fat), 111 mg chol., 415 mg sodium, 24 g carb., 8 g fiber, 41 g pro. Exchanges: 0.5 vegetable, 1 starch, 5 lean meat. Carb choices: 1.5.

Red Beans and Rice

If you like hot and spicy flavors, use the andouille sausage and the ¼ teaspoon cayenne pepper.

SERVINGS 6

CARB. PER SERVING 36 g

- 1 cup dry red kidney beans
- 1 smoked pork hock
- 12 ounces andouille sausage or cooked kielbasa, cut into ½-inch pieces
- 1½ cups water
- 1 cup reduced-sodium chicken broth
- 1 medium onion, chopped (½ cup)
- 1 stalk celery, chopped (½ cup)
- 1 tablespoon tomato paste
- 2 cloves garlic, minced
- ½ teaspoon dried thyme, crushed
- ½ teaspoon dried oregano, crushed
- ⅛ to ¼ teaspoon cayenne pepper
- 1 8.8-ounce package cooked long grain or brown rice
- ½ cup chopped red or yellow sweet pepper

1. Rinse beans. In a large saucepan, combine beans and 6 cups water. Bring to boiling; reduce heat. Simmer, uncovered, for 10 minutes. Remove from heat. Cover and let stand for 1 hour. Drain and rinse beans.

2. In a 3½- or 4-quart slow cooker, combine beans, pork hock, andouille, the 1½ cups water, the broth, onion, celery, tomato paste, garlic, thyme, oregano, and cayenne pepper.

3. Cover and cook on low-heat setting for 9 to 10 hours or on high-heat setting for 4½ to 5 hours.

4. Remove pork hock. When cool enough to handle, cut meat off bone; cut meat into bite-size pieces. Discard bone. Stir meat, rice, and sweet pepper into bean mixture in slow cooker. If using low-heat setting, turn to high-heat setting. Cover and cook for 30 minutes more.

PER SERVING: 262 cal., 5 g total fat (1 g sat. fat), 33 mg chol., 604 mg sodium, 36 g carb., 6 g fiber, 18 g pro. Exchanges: 2 starch, 1.5 medium-fat meat. Carb choices: 2.5.

Slow-cooking tip: Look for lamb foreshanks. Smaller than hind shanks, they're a perfect fit for the slow cooker. You may need to ask the butcher to order them.

Spicy Lamb Shanks

Spicy Lamb Shanks

Lamb shanks are an underutilized and wonderfully flavorful cut that is ideal for the slow cooker. The meat literally falls off the bone. Infused with orange and spices, it is the perfect warming supper for a chilly evening.

SERVINGS 6 (9¼ ounces meat with bone, ½ cup vegetables, and ¼ cup sauce each)

CARB. PER SERVING 17 g

2 large oranges
5 medium carrots, cut into 2-inch pieces
1½ cups frozen small whole onions
4 large cloves garlic, thinly sliced
4 meaty lamb shanks (about 4 pounds)
6 inches stick cinnamon, broken into 1-inch pieces
1¼ cups lower-sodium beef broth
1½ teaspoons ground cardamom
1 teaspoon ground cumin
½ teaspoon ground turmeric
½ teaspoon black pepper
2 tablespoons cold water
4 teaspoons cornstarch
⅓ cup pitted kalamata or other black olives, halved
1 tablespoon snipped fresh cilantro

1. Using a vegetable peeler, remove the peel from one of the oranges, avoiding the bitter white pith. Cut peel into thin strips (to yield about ¼ cup). Squeeze juice from both oranges to make about ⅔ cup. Set aside.

2. In a 5- to 6-quart slow cooker, combine carrots, onions, and garlic. Add orange peel strips, lamb shanks, and stick cinnamon. In a small bowl, stir together orange juice, beef broth, cardamom, cumin, turmeric, and pepper; pour over all in cooker.

3. Cover and cook on low-heat setting for 11 to 12 hours or on high-heat setting for 5½ to 6 hours. Remove stick cinnamon.

4. Using a slotted spoon, transfer meat and vegetables to a serving platter; keep warm.

5. For sauce, pour cooking liquid into a glass measuring cup; skim off fat. Measure 1½ cups of the cooking liquid. In a small saucepan, stir together the water and cornstarch until smooth. Stir in 1½ cups cooking liquid. Cook and stir over medium heat until thickened and bubbly; cook and stir for 2 minutes more. Serve sauce with meat and vegetables. Sprinkle with olives and cilantro.

PER SERVING: 223 cal., 5 g total fat (1 g sat. fat), 85 mg chol., 313 mg sodium, 17 g carb., 4 g fiber, 28 g pro. Exchanges: 1 vegetable, 0.5 carb., 3.5 lean meat. Carb choices: 1.

Lamb Shanks with Polenta

Look for quick-cooking polenta mix near the cornmeal and flour in the supermarket.

SERVINGS 6 (9 ounces meat with bone, ⅓ cup polenta, and about 3 tablespoons onion mixture each)

CARB. PER SERVING 36 g

1 pound boiling onions, peeled
½ cup pitted Greek black olives or other pitted black olives
4 meaty lamb shanks (about 4 pounds)
4 cloves garlic, minced
2 teaspoons dried rosemary, crushed
¼ teaspoon salt
¼ teaspoon black pepper
1 cup reduced-sodium chicken broth
¾ cup quick-cooking polenta mix
Snipped fresh Italian (flat-leaf) parsley (optional)

1. In a 5- to 6-quart slow cooker, combine onions and olives. Add lamb shanks. Sprinkle with garlic, rosemary, salt, and pepper. Pour broth over all in cooker.

2. Cover and cook on low-heat setting for 11 to 12 hours or on high-heat setting for 5½ to 6 hours.

3. Prepare polenta according to package directions, except use only ¼ teaspoon salt. Using a slotted spoon, transfer lamb, onions, and olives to a serving dish and pass with polenta. If desired, garnish with fresh parsley. If you wish to serve cooking liquid with meat, skim off fat; strain liquid before serving.

PER SERVING: 315 cal., 5 g total fat (1 g sat. fat), 85 mg chol., 488 mg sodium, 36 g carb., 5 g fiber, 31 g pro. Exchanges: 2 starch, 3.5 lean meat. Carb choices: 2.5.

Braised Lamb with Dill Sauce

Braised Lamb with Dill Sauce

Creamy yogurt-dill sauce tops tender lamb chops and new potatoes for a meal full of fresh flavor.
SERVINGS 3 (2 lamb chops, 1 cup vegetables, and about 1/3 cup sauce each)
CARB. PER SERVING 31 g

- 12 ounces tiny new potatoes
- 3 medium carrots, cut into 1-inch pieces
- 6 lamb rib chops, cut 3/4 to 1 inch thick
- 2 teaspoons cooking oil
- 3/4 cup water
- 2 teaspoons snipped fresh dill weed or 1/2 teaspoon dried dill weed
- 1/2 teaspoon salt
- 1/4 teaspoon black pepper
- 1/2 cup plain low-fat yogurt
- 4 teaspoons all-purpose flour
- 1/8 teaspoon salt
- 1/8 teaspoon black pepper
  Fresh dill weed (optional)

1. Remove a narrow strip of peel from the center of each potato. Place potatoes and carrots in a 3 1/2- or 4-quart slow cooker. In a large skillet, brown lamb chops, a few at a time, on both sides in hot oil. Drain off fat. Place lamb chops on vegetables in cooker. Add the water. Sprinkle with 1 teaspoon of the fresh or 1/4 teaspoon of the dried dill weed, 1/2 teaspoon salt, and 1/4 teaspoon pepper.
2. Cover and cook on low-heat setting for 7 to 8 hours or on high-heat setting for 3 1/2 to 4 hours.
3. Transfer chops and vegetables to a serving platter; cover to keep warm.
4. For sauce, strain cooking liquid into a glass measuring cup; skim off fat. Measure 1/2 cup cooking liquid. Combine yogurt and flour in a small saucepan. Stir in 1/2 cup cooking liquid, remaining 1 teaspoon fresh or 1/4 teaspoon dried dill weed, 1/8 teaspoon salt, and 1/8 teaspoon pepper. Cook and stir over medium heat until thickened and bubbly; cook and stir for 1 minute more. Serve chops and vegetables with sauce. If desired, garnish with fresh dill weed.
PER SERVING: 367 cal., 13 g total fat (5 g sat. fat), 84 mg chol., 469 mg sodium, 31 g carb., 4 g fiber, 30 g pro. Exchanges: 0.5 vegetable, 3.5 lean meat, 1 fat. Carb choices: 2.

Lentil-and-Rice
Stuffed Peppers

Lentil-and-Rice Stuffed Peppers

Cooking the peppers for a couple of minutes in boiling water takes off the chill and gives them slight tenderness.
SERVINGS 8 (1 pepper half and about 1 cup lentil mixture each)
CARB. PER SERVING 39 g

- 1 1/2 cups chopped carrots
- 1 1/2 cups chopped celery (3 stalks)
- 1 cup dry brown lentils, rinsed and drained
- 2/3 cup uncooked brown rice
- 2 tablespoons yellow mustard
- 1 tablespoon packed brown sugar
- 1 14-ounce can vegetable broth
- 2 1/4 cups water
- 1 15-ounce can tomato sauce with garlic and onion
- 2 tablespoons cider vinegar
- 4 red and/or green sweet peppers
  Snipped fresh Italian (flat-leaf) parsley (optional)

1. In a 3 1/2- or 4-quart slow cooker, combine carrots, celery, lentils, uncooked rice, mustard, and brown sugar. Stir in vegetable broth and the water.
2. Cover and cook on high-heat setting for 3 to 3 1/2 hours. Stir in tomato sauce and vinegar. Cover and cook for 30 minutes more.
3. Halve sweet peppers lengthwise; remove seeds and membranes.* To serve, spoon lentil mixture in and around pepper halves. If desired, sprinkle with parsley.
*TEST KITCHEN TIP: If desired, in a Dutch oven, cook sweet pepper halves in a large amount of boiling water about 3 minutes or until crisp-tender. Drain well.
PER SERVING: 203 cal., 1 g total fat (0 g sat. fat), 0 mg chol., 511 mg sodium, 39 g carb., 11 g fiber, 9 g pro. Exchanges: 1.5 vegetable, 2 starch. Carb choices: 2.5.

cook once, eat again

Cider-Braised Pork
Roast and Apples

Cooking in big batches has its appeal, but who likes eating the same thing night after night? Turn to your slow cooker to prepare something ultimately tender and fabulously flavorful today, and then have enough to fix something deliciously different for dinner tomorrow.

now

Cider-Braised Pork Roast and Apples

Pork and apples, a classic pairing, cook up beautifully in the slow cooker.

SERVINGS 6 (about 3½ ounces meat and 4 apple wedges each) + reserves

CARB. PER SERVING 23 g

1   3-pound boneless pork top loin roast
½   teaspoon salt
½   teaspoon dried thyme, crushed
½   teaspoon dried sage, crushed
¼   teaspoon black pepper
2   tablespoons cooking oil
4   red, yellow, and/or green apples, cored and each cut into 6 wedges
⅓   cup chopped shallots
6   cloves garlic, minced
3   tablespoons quick-cooking tapioca
¾   cup reduced-sodium chicken broth
¾   cup apple cider or juice

1. Trim fat from roast. In a small bowl, stir together salt, thyme, sage, and pepper. Sprinkle spice mixture over roast; rub in with your fingers. In a large skillet, brown roast on all sides in hot oil over medium heat.
2. In a 6- to 7-quart slow cooker, place apples, shallots, and garlic; sprinkle with tapioca. Place roast on top of apple mixture. Pour broth and apple cider over roast.
3. Cover and cook on low-heat setting for 8 to 10 hours or high-heat setting for 4 to 5 hours.
4. Reserve and store* 1 pound of the meat for Pork and Berry Salad (page 34). Slice remaining pork. Spoon some of the cooking liquid over pork and apples to serve.

*TO STORE: Place meat in an airtight container; cover. Chill for up to 3 days or freeze for up to 3 months. Thaw in refrigerator overnight before using.

PER SERVING: 285 cal., 8 g total fat (2 g sat. fat), 70 mg chol., 258 mg sodium, 23 g carb., 2 g fiber, 29 g pro. Exchanges: 1.5 fruit, 4 lean meat, 0.5 fat. Carb choices: 1.5.

Fresh berries require little prep. Simply give them a quick rinse under cold running water just before you're ready to eat them.

later

Pork and Berry Salad

Partnered with sweet berries, leftover pork hits a home run in this main-dish salad. The salad looks pretty when the pork is sliced, but chopped meat may be easier to eat.

SERVINGS 6
CARB. PER SERVING 11 g

Reserved meat from Cider-Braised Pork Roast and Apples (page 33)
6   cups torn mixed greens
3   cups mixed berries, such as sliced strawberries, blueberries, and/or raspberries
½   cup bottled reduced-calorie balsamic vinaigrette or other vinaigrette

1. Chop or slice meat. Arrange 1 cup of greens on each of six serving plates. Top each with about 2½ ounces meat and ½ cup berries. Drizzle each with about 1½ tablespoons vinaigrette.

PER SERVING: 221 cal., 9 g total fat (2 g sat. fat), 56 mg chol., 229 mg sodium, 11 g carb., 2 g fiber, 23 g pro. Exchanges: 1 vegetable, 0.5 fruit, 3 lean meat, 1 fat. Carb choices: 1.

Salad Sampler

If berries are not in season or the price is more prime than you're willing to pay, try one of these fresh options instead.

1. **Add** slices of fresh pear and a light sprinkling of crumbled blue cheese.
2. **Try** fresh peach slices and a few chopped toasted almonds.
3. **Use** chopped apple and thinly sliced red onion.
4. **Toss in** a handful of grape tomatoes.
5. **Chill** cooked green beans and toss them in.
6. **Arrange** chilled cooked asparagus spears on top of the greens.
7. **Stir in** some fresh plum wedges.
8. **Add** strips of sweet pepper along with a little reduced-fat feta cheese.
9. **Try** a few dried tart red cherries or cranberries.
10. **Sprinkle** with a combo of chopped red onion and sliced fresh mushrooms.

Pork and Berry Salad

Sage-Scented
Pork Chops

Sage-Scented Pork Chops

*Just before serving, boost the flavor of the cooking
liquid with two simple stir-ins: Dijon-style mustard
and caraway seeds.*

SERVINGS 6 (1 pork chop, $1/2$ cup vegetable
mixture, and $1/4$ cup sauce each) + reserves

CARB. PER SERVING 12 g

10 boneless pork loin chops, cut $3/4$ inch thick (about
    $3^1/2$ pounds)

2 teaspoons dried sage, crushed

1 teaspoon black pepper

$1/2$ teaspoon salt

2 tablespoons cooking oil

1 medium onion, thinly sliced

$1/2$ cup reduced-sodium chicken broth

$1/3$ cup dry white wine or apple juice

3 tablespoons quick-cooking tapioca, crushed

$1/2$ of a medium head green cabbage, cut into $1/2$-inch strips

1 tablespoon Dijon-style mustard

1 teaspoon caraway seeds

Black pepper

Fresh sage sprigs (optional)

1. Trim fat from chops. In a small bowl, stir together
sage, 1 teaspoon pepper, and the salt. Rub sage mixture
onto one side of each chop. In a very large skillet, brown
both sides of chops, half at a time, in hot oil over
medium heat.

2. In a 6- to 7-quart slow cooker, place onion, broth,
wine, and tapioca. Add the browned chops to cooker.
Top with cabbage.

3. Cover and cook on low-heat setting for 4 to 5 hours or
on high-heat setting for 2 to $2^1/2$ hours.

4. Reserve and store* 4 chops for Cheesy Meat and
Potato Casserole (page 37). Transfer remaining
6 chops to a platter; cover to keep warm. Using a slotted
spoon, transfer cabbage and onion to a serving bowl.
Stir mustard and caraway seeds into remaining liquid
in cooker. Season sauce to taste with pepper. Spoon
sauce over pork and cabbage. If desired, garnish with
fresh sage.

*TO STORE: Place chops in an airtight container; cover. Chill
for up to 3 days or freeze for up to 3 months. Thaw in
refrigerator overnight before using.

PER SERVING: 324 cal., 15 g total fat (5 g sat. fat), 102 mg chol.,
345 mg sodium, 12 g carb., 2 g fiber, 32 g pro. Exchanges:
1 vegetable, 0.5 starch, 4 lean meat, 1.5 fat. Carb
choices: 1.

Cheesy Meat and Potato Casserole

Leftover home-style pork chops go gourmet in this bubbly hot, rich, and delish dish.

SERVINGS 6 (about 1 cup each)
CARB. PER SERVING 17 g

Nonstick cooking spray
1 pound round red or Yukon gold potatoes, cut into ½-inch-thick wedges
5 green onions, thinly sliced
2 cloves garlic, minced
½ of an 8-ounce package reduced-fat cream cheese (Neufchâtel), cut up
2 tablespoons Dijon-style mustard
1 teaspoon snipped fresh sage or ½ teaspoon dried sage, crushed
¾ cup fat-free milk
Reserved pork chops from Sage-Scented Pork Chops (page 36), cubed
1 cup jarred roasted red sweet peppers, drained and thinly sliced
¾ cup shredded Gruyère or Swiss cheese (3 ounces)

1. Preheat oven to 350°F. Coat a 2-quart square baking dish with cooking spray; set aside. In a large saucepan, cook potatoes, covered, in enough lightly salted boiling water to cover for 10 to 12 minutes or just until tender. Drain and set aside.

2. For sauce, coat a medium saucepan with cooking spray; heat over medium heat. Add 4 of the green onions and the garlic to saucepan. Cook for 3 to 5 minutes or until onions are tender, stirring frequently. Remove from heat. Add cream cheese, mustard, and sage to onion mixture. Stir until cheese is melted and smooth. Gradually add milk, stirring until smooth.

3. Layer half of the potato wedges in prepared baking dish. Top with half of the pork chops, half of the red peppers, half of the sauce, and half of the Gruyère cheese. Repeat layers once except do not top with remaining Gruyère cheese.

4. Bake, covered, for 20 minutes. Uncover and top with remaining Gruyère cheese. Bake for 5 to 10 minutes more or until heated through and cheese is starting to brown. Let stand 10 minutes. Sprinkle with remaining sliced green onion before serving.

PER SERVING: 362 cal., 19 g total fat (8 g sat. fat), 98 mg chol., 400 mg sodium, 17 g carb., 2 g fiber, 29 g pro. Exchanges: 0.5 vegetable, 1 starch, 4 lean meat, 2 fat. Carb choices: 1.

Cheesy Meat and Potato Casserole

Kickin' Chicken Chili

Here's a chili with some flexibility. Substitute red beans for white or red salsa for green.

SERVINGS 6 (1 cup each) + reserves
CARB. PER SERVING 16 g

- 2 pounds skinless, boneless chicken breast halves or thighs, cut into 1-inch pieces
- 2 teaspoons ground cumin
- 1 tablespoon olive oil or cooking oil
- 1 16-ounce jar green salsa
- 1 16-ounce package frozen stir-fry vegetables (green, red, and yellow sweet peppers and onions)
- 1 15-ounce can cannellini beans (white kidney beans), rinsed and drained
- 1 14.5-ounce can no-salt-added diced tomatoes
- 1 medium onion, chopped (½ cup)
- 2 cloves garlic, minced

1. Toss chicken with cumin. In a large skillet, cook chicken, half at a time, in hot oil over medium heat until no longer pink. Drain off fat. Place chicken in a 4- to 5-quart slow cooker. Stir in salsa, vegetables, beans, undrained tomatoes, onion, and garlic.

2. Cover and cook on low-heat setting for 4 to 5 hours or on high-heat setting for 2 to 2½ hours.

3. Reserve and store* 3 cups of the chili for in Kickin' Chicken Taco Salad (right). Serve remaining chili.

*TO STORE: Place chili in an airtight container; cover. Chill for up to 3 days.

PER SERVING: 197 cal., 3 g total fat (1 g sat. fat), 57 mg chol., 352 mg sodium, 16 g carb., 5 g fiber, 27 g pro. Exchanges: 1 vegetable, 0.5 starch, 3.5 lean meat. Carb choices: 1.

Kickin' Chicken Chili

Kickin' Chicken Taco Salad

Olé! A bowl of chili turns a basic salad into a fun, fiesta-style meal.

SERVINGS 6 (1⅓ cups each)
CARB. PER SERVING 26 g

Reserved Kickin' Chicken Chili (left)
- 6 cups torn green leaf lettuce
- 1 large avocado, halved, seeded, peeled, and chopped

1 cup grape tomatoes or cherry tomatoes, halved
   if desired
1 medium red onion, chopped (½ cup)
1½ cups coarsely crushed baked tortilla chips
   Cilantro Sour Cream (right) (optional)

1. In a medium saucepan, heat reserved chili over medium-low heat until hot. In a very large bowl, combine lettuce, avocado, tomatoes, and red onion. Add heated chili; toss to combine.

2. Divide among six salad bowls. Sprinkle with chips. If desired, spoon Cilantro Sour Cream evenly onto salads.

CILANTRO SOUR CREAM: In a small bowl, stir together ¼ cup light sour cream and 2 tablespoons snipped fresh cilantro.

PER SERVING: 218 cal., 7 g total fat (1 g sat. fat), 29 mg chol., 290 mg sodium, 26 g carb., 6 g fiber, 16 g pro. Exchanges: 1.5 vegetable, 1 starch, 1.5 lean meat, 0.5 fat. Carb choices: 2.

Indian-Spiced Chicken Thighs

At first glance, some Indian-inspired recipes look so long! But take another look—many of the ingredients are spices, which take very little time to measure but add so much pleasure.

SERVINGS 6 (about 2 thighs, about $1/3$ cup sauce, and $1/2$ cup rice each) + reserves

CARB. PER SERVING 33 g

2	cups thinly sliced onions (4 medium)
$1/4$	cup quick-cooking tapioca
8	cloves garlic, minced
24	to 30 skinless, boneless chicken thighs (4 to $4^{1}/2$ pounds)
1	tablespoon ground cumin
2	teaspoons curry powder
$1^{1}/2$	teaspoons salt
$1^{1}/2$	teaspoons ground coriander
$1/2$	teaspoon ground cinnamon
$1/4$	teaspoon ground cloves
$1/4$	teaspoon cayenne pepper
$1/4$	teaspoon black pepper
1	14-ounce can reduced-sodium chicken broth
1	6-ounce carton plain yogurt
3	cups hot cooked basmati rice
	Snipped fresh mint (optional)
	Finely shredded lemon peel (optional)
3	tablespoons toasted slivered almonds (optional)

1. Place onions in a 5- to 7-quart slow cooker; sprinkle with tapioca and garlic. Top with chicken. Sprinkle with cumin, curry powder, salt, coriander, cinnamon, cloves, cayenne pepper, and black pepper. Pour broth over all in cooker.

2. Cover and cook on low-heat setting for 7 to 8 hours or on high-heat setting for $3^{1}/2$ to 4 hours.

3. Reserve and store* half of the chicken thighs (12 to 15) and half of the onion mixture (about 2 cups) for Coconut Chicken and Couscous (page 41). Transfer remaining chicken to a serving platter; cover to keep warm. Whisk yogurt into remaining onion mixture in cooker. Serve chicken and yogurt sauce with hot cooked basmati rice. If desired, sprinkle with fresh mint, lemon peel, and slivered almonds.

***TO STORE:** Cut chicken into $3/4$-inch pieces; place chicken and onion mixture (about $5^{1}/2$ cups) in an airtight container; cover. Chill for up to 3 days.

PER SERVING: 337 cal., 6 g total fat (2 g sat. fat), 127 mg chol., 602 mg sodium, 33 g carb., 1 g fiber, 35 g pro. Exchanges: 2 starch, 4 lean meat. Carb choices: 2.

If you're looking to add a splash of color to this bowl of earth tones, try golden raisins or snipped dried apricots instead of the regular raisins. And add a sprinkling of snipped fresh basil or cilantro.

later

Coconut Chicken and Couscous

Add a can of nutty-good coconut milk and a little extra spice to the reserves from Indian-Spiced Chicken Thighs, and you'll have tonight's equally intriguing meal ready in minutes.

SERVINGS 6 (about 1 cup chicken mixture and ⅓ cup couscous each)
CARB. PER SERVING 28 g

Reserved chicken and onion mixture from Indian-Spiced Chicken Thighs (page 40)
1 13.5- or 14-ounce can unsweetened light coconut milk
4 teaspoons cornstarch
½ teaspoon curry powder
2 tablespoons raisins
2 cups hot cooked whole wheat couscous
2 tablespoons toasted shredded coconut (optional)

1. In a large saucepan, heat reserved chicken and onion mixture over medium heat until hot. In a medium bowl, stir together coconut milk, cornstarch, and curry powder; stir into chicken mixture. Stir in raisins.
2. Cook and stir over medium heat until thickened and bubbly; cook and stir for 2 minutes more. Serve with hot cooked couscous. If desired, sprinkle with toasted coconut.
PER SERVING: 334 cal., 10 g total fat (4 g sat. fat), 125 mg chol., 440 mg sodium, 28 g carb., 3 g fiber, 33 g pro. Exchanges: 2 starch, 3.5 lean meat, 0.5 fat. Carb choices: 2.

Coconut Chicken and Couscous

Wine-Braised
Beef Brisket

now

Wine-Braised Beef Brisket

If you have liquid smoke, add a splash to the sauce—it will imbue the flavor and color with richness.

SERVINGS 6 (about 3 ounces meat, ¹/₂ cup carrots, and ¹/₂ cup potatoes each) + reserves

CARB. PER SERVING 31 g

- 1   3-pound fresh beef brisket
- 6   medium carrots, bias-sliced in 2-inch lengths (3 cups)
- 1   large onion, finely chopped (1 cup)
- ³/₄   cup dry red wine
- ¹/₄   cup no-salt-added tomato paste*
- 4   teaspoons quick-cooking tapioca
- 2   teaspoons Worcestershire sauce
- 1   teaspoon chili powder
- 1   teaspoon liquid smoke (optional)
- ¹/₂   teaspoon garlic powder
- 3   cups hot cooked mashed potatoes

1. Trim fat from brisket. If necessary, cut beef to fit in a 5- to 6-quart slow cooker. Place carrots and onion in cooker. Top with brisket. In a medium bowl, combine wine, tomato paste, tapioca, Worcestershire sauce, chili powder, liquid smoke (if using), garlic powder, and ¹/₄ teaspoon *salt*; pour over all in cooker.

2. Cover and cook on low-heat setting for 9 to 11 hours or on high-heat setting for 4¹/₂ to 5¹/₂ hours.

3. Remove brisket from cooker. Using a slotted spoon, remove vegetables from cooker. Reserve and store** 8 ounces of the beef and ¹/₂ cup of the cooking liquid for Beef-Mushroom Pizza (page 43). Slice remaining beef; serve with vegetables, remaining cooking liquid, and mashed potatoes.

*TEST KITCHEN TIP: Transfer remaining tomato paste from 6-ounce can to an airtight storage container; cover and chill for up to 3 days. Use in Beef-Mushroom Pizza (page 43).

**TO STORE: Place beef in an airtight container. Place cooking liquid in a second airtight container. Cover and chill for up to 3 days.

PER SERVING: 333 cal., 9 g total fat (3 g sat. fat), 45 mg chol., 503 mg sodium, 31 g carb., 5 g fiber, 28 g pro. Exchanges: 1 vegetable, 1.5 starch, 3 lean meat, 1 fat. Carb choices: 2.

Beef-Mushroom Pizza

Transform leftover brisket into a delightfully hearty bistro-style pizza.

SERVINGS 6 (1 wedge each)
CARB. PER SERVING 28 g

1 12-inch whole wheat Italian bread shell (such as Boboli® brand)
Reserved no-salt-added tomato paste from Wine-Braised Beef Brisket (page 42)
Reserved beef and cooking liquid from Wine-Braised Beef Brisket (page 42)
1 cup sliced fresh mushrooms
½ cup chopped green sweet pepper
¾ cup shredded reduced-fat mozzarella cheese (3 ounces)

1. Preheat oven to 425°F. Place bread shell on a large pizza pan or baking sheet; set aside. In a small bowl, whisk together tomato paste and the reserved cooking liquid. Chop the reserved beef.
2. Spread tomato paste mixture over bread shell. Top with beef, mushrooms, sweet pepper, and cheese. Bake for 12 to 15 minutes or until heated through and cheese is melted. Cut into 6 wedges to serve.

PER SERVING: 282 cal., 8 g total fat (4 g sat. fat), 34 mg chol., 478 mg sodium, 28 g carb., 5 g fiber, 25 g pro. Exchanges: 1 vegetable, 1.5 starch, 2.5 lean meat, 0.5 fat. Carb choices: 2.

Cook tender, juicy chicken thighs along with a few aromatic herbs and spices in your slow cooker, then shred the chicken to use in divinely delicious dinners for days to follow.

now

Shredded Chicken Master Recipe

Chicken thighs stay moist and flavorful when slow-cooked.

SERVINGS 12 (¹/₂ cup each); 6 cups total
CARB. PER SERVING 0 g

- 4¹/₂ to 5 pounds chicken thighs, skinned
- 4 fresh thyme sprigs
- 4 fresh parsley stems
- 2 bay leaves
- 2 cloves garlic, halved
- ¹/₂ teaspoon whole black peppercorns
- 1 32-ounce box reduced-sodium chicken broth

1. Place chicken thighs in a 4- to 5-quart slow cooker. For the bouquet garni, cut an 8-inch square from a double thickness of 100-percent-cotton cheesecloth. Place thyme sprigs, parsley stems, bay leaves, garlic, and peppercorns in center of the cheesecloth square. Gather corners together and tie with 100-percent-cotton kitchen string. Add bouquet garni to slow cooker. Pour broth over all.

2. Cover and cook on low-heat setting for 7 to 8 hours or on high-heat setting for 3¹/₂ to 4 hours. Discard the bouquet garni.

3. Using a slotted spoon, transfer chicken to a large bowl. When chicken is cool enough to handle, remove meat from bones. Using two forks, shred meat. Add enough of the cooking juices to moisten meat. Strain and reserve cooking juices to use for chicken stock. Place 2-cup portions of chicken and chicken stock in separate airtight containers; cover. Chill for up to 3 days or freeze for up to 3 months.

PER SERVING: 115 cal., 4 g total fat (1 g sat. fat), 80 mg chol., 114 mg sodium, 0 g carb., 0 g fiber, 19 g pro. Exchanges: 2.5 lean meat. Carb choices: 0.

later

Greek-Style Chicken Salad

This chilled chicken salad makes a great lunch. For toting, assemble each salad in an airtight container and pack in an insulated bag with an ice pack.

SERVINGS 4
CARB. PER SERVING 13 g

- 2 cups Shredded Chicken Master Recipe (left)
- ¹/₂ cup bottled reduced-calorie Greek vinaigrette salad dressing
- 1 teaspoon finely shredded lemon peel
- ¹/₂ teaspoon dried oregano, crushed
- 6 cups torn romaine lettuce
- 1 medium cucumber, chopped (1¹/₃ cups)
- 1 cup grape tomatoes, halved
- 1 medium yellow sweet pepper, chopped (³/₄ cup)
- 1 medium red onion, thinly sliced and separated into rings
- ¹/₂ cup crumbled reduced-fat feta cheese (2 ounces)
- ¹/₄ cup pitted kalamata olives, halved
- Lemon wedges (optional)

1. In a medium bowl, combine chicken, ¹/₄ cup of the vinaigrette, the lemon peel, and oregano; set aside.

2. In a large salad bowl, toss lettuce with remaining ¹/₄ cup vinaigrette. Divide lettuce among four shallow bowls. Top each with cucumber, tomatoes, sweet pepper, and onion. Add chicken mixture to the center of each salad. Sprinkle with feta cheese and olives. If desired, serve with lemon wedges.

PER SERVING: 220 cal., 8 g total fat (3 g sat. fat), 85 mg chol., 481 mg sodium, 13 g carb., 4 g fiber, 25 g pro. Exchanges: 2.5 vegetable, 2.5 lean meat, 1 fat. Carb choices: 1.

Greek-Style Chicken Salad

Apricot-Mustard Chicken Sandwiches

Peanut Noodles with
Chicken and Vegetables

Bulk Up on Veggies

Vegetables are high in fiber and
loaded with vitamins and nutrients.
They also serve as a great filler, so
sneak a few extra into your daily diet.

1. **Snack** on celery.
2. **Toss** a few broccoli florets
   into a lettuce salad.
3. **Add** leafy greens to a
   sandwich.
4. **Layer** ribbons of zucchini
   on a burger.
5. **Pop** a few grape tomatoes
   as a snack.
6. **Try** cooked beets with a
   sprinkling of reduced-fat
   feta cheese as a side.
7. **Chomp** on crunchy
   cauliflower florets instead
   of chips.
8. **Toss** handfuls of fresh
   spinach into your favorite
   pasta dish.
9. **Crunch** on sweet peppers
   when you're craving
   something sweet.
10. **Munch** on fresh
    mushrooms between
    meals.

later

Apricot-Mustard Chicken Sandwiches

If you have a bag of baby spinach on hand, add a healthy dose of the nutrient-loaded greens to these sandwiches along with the onion slices.

SERVINGS 4 (1 sandwich each)
CARB. PER SERVING 30 g

- 1 cup finely chopped onion (1 medium)
- 2 cloves garlic, minced
- 1 tablespoon cooking oil
- 2 cups Shredded Chicken Master Recipe (page 44)
- 3 tablespoons spicy brown mustard
- 3 tablespoons low-sugar apricot preserves
- 1 tablespoon cider vinegar
- 1 tablespoon bourbon (optional)
- ¼ teaspoon cayenne pepper
- 4 whole wheat hamburger buns, split and toasted
- 4 thin slices red onion (optional)

1. In a large skillet, cook chopped onion and garlic in hot oil over medium heat about 4 minutes or until tender. Stir in shredded chicken, mustard, apricot preserves, vinegar, bourbon, and cayenne pepper. Heat through. Simmer, uncovered, about 5 minutes or until desired consistency.
2. Spoon about ½ cup chicken mixture onto each bun bottom. If desired, top with red onion slices. Add bun tops.

PER SERVING: 304 cal., 8 g total fat (1 g sat. fat), 80 mg chol., 506 mg sodium, 30 g carb., 3 g fiber, 24 g pro. Exchanges: 2 starch, 2.5 lean meat, 1 fat. Carb choices: 2.

later

Peanut Noodles with Chicken and Vegetables

There's no fussing here—a sprinkling of peanuts and green onions gives this flavor-loaded noodle bowl a fast finish.

SERVINGS 6 (1 cup each)
CARB. PER SERVING 29 g

- 6 ounces dried multigrain spaghetti
- 1 16-ounce package frozen sugar snap stir-fry vegetable blend
- 3 tablespoons creamy peanut butter
- 1 tablespoon sugar
- 2 tablespoons reduced-sodium soy sauce
- 2 tablespoons water
- 1 tablespoon vegetable oil
- 2 cloves garlic, minced
- ¼ teaspoon crushed red pepper
- 2 cups Shredded Chicken Master Recipe (page 44)
- ⅓ cup chopped peanuts and/or sliced green onions

1. In a 4-quart Dutch oven, cook spaghetti according to package directions, adding vegetables for the last 2 minutes of cooking time; drain.
2. Meanwhile, in a small saucepan, combine peanut butter, sugar, soy sauce, the water, vegetable oil, garlic, and crushed red pepper. Heat until peanut butter is melted and sugar is dissolved, stirring frequently.
3. In a large bowl, combine pasta mixture, peanut sauce, and shredded chicken. Toss well to coat. Serve immediately. If desired, top with chopped peanuts and/or sliced green onions.

PER SERVING: 289 cal., 9 g total fat (2 g sat. fat), 54 mg chol., 341 mg sodium, 29 g carb., 4 g fiber, 21 g pro. Exchanges: 1 vegetable, 1.5 starch, 2 lean meat, 1 fat. Carb choices: 2.

Pulled Pork Master Recipe

*Despite being one of the most economical cuts of meat,
pork shoulder delivers the ultimate in flavor.*

SERVINGS 12 ($^{1}/_{2}$ cup each); 6 cups total
CARB. PER SERVING 7 g

- 3 to 3$^{1}/_{2}$ pounds boneless pork shoulder
- 1 large sweet onion, such as Vidalia, Walla Walla, or Maui, chopped (1 cup)
- 6 cloves garlic, minced
- 1 cup bottled chili sauce
- 2 tablespoons packed brown sugar
- 2 tablespoons cider vinegar
- 1 tablespoon Worcestershire sauce
- 1 tablespoon chili powder
- $^{1}/_{2}$ teaspoon black pepper

1. Trim fat from meat. If necessary, cut meat to fit in a 4- to 5-quart slow cooker. Place meat, onion, and garlic in slow cooker. In a medium bowl, combine chili sauce, brown sugar, cider vinegar, Worcestershire sauce, chili powder, and pepper. Pour over all in cooker.
2. Cover and cook on low-heat setting for 10 to 11 hours or on high-heat setting for 5 to 6 hours. Remove meat from cooker, reserving cooking liquid. Using two forks, shred meat, discarding fat. Skim fat from liquid. Add enough liquid to the meat to moisten. Place 2-cup portions of pork in airtight containers; cover. Chill for up to 3 days or freeze for up to 3 months.
PER SERVING: 187 cal., 7 g total fat (2 g sat. fat), 73 mg chol., 359 mg sodium, 7 g carb., 0 g fiber, 23 g pro. Exchanges: 0.5 carb., 3 lean meat, 0.5 fat. Carb choices: 0.5.

Mole Pork and Green Olive Quesadillas

*Chocolate chips in a quesadilla recipe? You bet.
Mole (MOH-lay), a rich dark sauce made from onion,
garlic, chiles, and chocolate, is one of Mexican
cuisine's greatest treasures.*

SERVINGS 6 (1 quesadilla each)
CARB. PER SERVING 28 g

- 1 large onion, chopped (1 cup)
- 3 cloves garlic, minced
- 2 teaspoons olive oil
- 2 teaspoons chili powder
- $^{1}/_{2}$ teaspoon ground cumin
- $^{1}/_{4}$ teaspoon ground cinnamon
- $^{1}/_{4}$ teaspoon dried oregano, crushed
- 2 teaspoons all-purpose flour
- $^{1}/_{3}$ cup water
- 2 tablespoons semisweet chocolate pieces
- 2 cups Pulled Pork Master Recipe (left)
- 6 8-inch flour tortillas
  Nonstick cooking spray
- $^{3}/_{4}$ cup shredded reduced-fat Monterey Jack cheese (3 ounces)
- 1 medium red onion, thinly sliced
- 3 tablespoons sliced pimiento-stuffed green olives

1. In a large skillet, cook chopped onion and garlic in hot oil over medium heat about 4 minutes or until tender. Stir in chili powder, cumin, cinnamon, and oregano; cook and stir for 1 minute more. Stir in flour. Stir in the water all at once. Cook until thickened and bubbly, stirring constantly. Stir in chocolate until melted. Stir in shredded pork and heat through.
2. Coat one side of each tortilla with cooking spray. Place tortillas, sprayed sides down, on cutting board or waxed paper. Sprinkle cheese over half of each tortilla. Top evenly with pork mixture, red onion slices, and green olives. Fold tortillas in half, pressing gently.
3. Heat a large nonstick skillet over medium heat. Cook quesadillas, two at a time, in hot skillet over medium heat for 4 to 6 minutes or until lightly browned, turning once. Remove quesadillas from skillet; place on a baking sheet. Keep warm in a 300°F oven. Repeat with remaining quesadillas. To serve, cut each quesadilla into three wedges.
PER SERVING: 340 cal., 16 g total fat (5 g sat. fat), 59 mg chol., 552 mg sodium, 28 g carb., 2 g fiber, 22 g pro. Exchanges: 2 starch, 2 lean meat, 2 fat. Carb choices: 2.

Mole Pork and
Green Olive Quesadillas

Shredded Pork and
Green Chile Roll-Ups

Shredded Pork and Green Chile Roll-Ups

A poblano chile can range from mild to somewhat snappy. Choose darker peppers for richer flavor.

SERVINGS 6 (1 roll-up each)
CARB. PER SERVING 25 g

 1 large onion, thinly sliced and separated into rings
 ½ of a fresh poblano chile pepper, chopped (see tip, page 55)
 1 tablespoon cooking oil
 2 cups Pulled Pork Master Recipe (page 48)
 6 8-inch whole wheat flour tortillas, warmed (see tip, page 52)
 ¾ cup chopped tomato
 ½ cup shredded reduced-fat cheddar cheese (2 ounces)
 ⅓ cup light sour cream
 3 tablespoons snipped fresh cilantro

1. In a large skillet, cook onion and poblano pepper in hot oil over medium heat about 5 minutes or until tender, stirring occasionally. Stir in shredded pork. Cook and stir for 2 to 3 minutes or until heated through.

2. Spoon pork mixture onto each tortilla. Top each with tomato, cheese, sour cream, and cilantro. Roll up tortillas. If desired, cut in half to serve.

PER SERVING: 334 cal., 13 g total fat (5 g sat. fat), 58 mg chol., 639 mg sodium, 25 g carb., 11 g fiber, 27 g pro. Exchanges: 0.5 vegetable, 1.5 starch, 3 lean meat, 1.5 fat. Carb choices: 1.5.

Asian Pork Wraps

Napa cabbage, sometimes labeled Chinese cabbage, and bok choy are not the same vegetable but are kitchen cousins. Either one adds fresh crunch and color to these wraps.

SERVINGS 8 (1 wrap each)
CARB. PER SERVING 27 g

 1 16-ounce package frozen stir-fry vegetables
 1 tablespoon olive oil
 2 cups Pulled Pork Master Recipe (page 48)
 ⅓ cup bottled hoisin sauce
 1 teaspoon ground ginger
 ½ teaspoon garlic powder
 8 8-inch whole wheat flour tortillas, warmed (see tip, page 52)
 1½ cups shredded or coarsely chopped napa cabbage or bok choy

1. In a large skillet, cook stir-fry vegetables in hot oil over medium-high heat for 4 to 5 minutes or until nearly tender. Drain excess liquid from the pan. Add shredded pork, hoisin sauce, ginger, and garlic powder. Cook and stir until heated through.

2. Arrange meat and vegetable mixture along center of each tortilla. Top with shredded cabbage. Fold bottom edges of tortillas up and over the filling. Roll up, beginning on one of the sides. If desired, secure with wooden toothpicks.

PER SERVING: 285 cal., 9 g total fat (2 g sat. fat), 37 mg chol., 688 mg sodium, 27 g carb., 12 g fiber, 21 g pro. Exchanges: 0.5 vegetable, 1.5 starch, 2.5 lean meat, 1 fat. Carb choices: 2.

Asian Pork Wraps

Shredded Beef Master Recipe

Pull out your slow cooker once and feed off the fabulous fixings for days to follow.

SERVINGS 12 ($^1/_2$ cup each); 6 cups total
CARB. PER SERVING 3 g

> 3 to 3$^1/_2$ pounds boneless beef chuck pot roast
> 2 large onions, cut into thin wedges
> 2 cloves garlic, minced
> 1 14-ounce can lower-sodium beef broth
> 1 tablespoon Worcestershire sauce
> 2 teaspoons dry mustard
> 1 teaspoon dried thyme, crushed
> $^1/_4$ teaspoon salt
> $^1/_4$ teaspoon cayenne pepper

1. Trim fat from roast. If necessary, cut roast to fit in a 4- to 5-quart slow cooker. Place onions and garlic in the cooker. Top with roast. In a medium bowl, combine broth, Worcestershire sauce, mustard, thyme, salt, and cayenne pepper. Pour over all in cooker.
2. Cover and cook on low-heat setting for 11 to 12 hours or on high-heat setting for 5$^1/_2$ to 6 hours.
3. Remove meat from cooker; remove onions with a slotted spoon, reserving cooking liquid. Using two forks, shred meat, discarding fat. Skim fat from liquid. Add onions to meat; add enough liquid to the meat mixture to moisten. Place 2-cup portions of beef in airtight containers; cover. Chill for up to 3 days or freeze for up to 3 months.
PER SERVING: 162 cal., 5 g total fat (2 g sat. fat), 50 mg chol., 146 mg sodium, 3 g carb., 0 g fiber, 26 g pro. Exchanges: 3.5 lean meat. Carb choices: 0.

Shredded Beef, Bean, and Corn Fajitas

Just when you thought you had experienced every kind of take on fajitas, here comes a really head-turning version. The something-extra secret is in the crunchy veggie topping.

SERVINGS 6 (1 fajita each)
CARB. PER SERVING 48 g

> 1 small red onion, cut into thin wedges
> 2 cloves garlic, minced
> 1 tablespoon olive oil
> 2 cups Shredded Beef Master Recipe (left)
> 1 14.5-ounce can Mexican-style stewed tomatoes, cut up
> $^3/_4$ cup frozen whole kernel corn
> $^3/_4$ cup canned black beans, rinsed and drained
> 2 teaspoons chili powder
> 1 small cucumber, seeded and chopped ($^1/_2$ cup)
> $^1/_2$ cup peeled and chopped jicama
> 1 tablespoon snipped fresh cilantro
> 6 7- to 8-inch flour tortillas, warmed
> $^1/_2$ cup light sour cream and/or purchased guacamole (optional)

1. In a large skillet, cook onion and garlic in hot oil over medium heat about 4 minutes or until tender. Stir in shredded beef, undrained tomatoes, corn, beans, and chili powder. Bring to boiling; reduce heat. Simmer, uncovered, about 5 minutes or until heated through and desired consistency.
2. Meanwhile, in a small bowl, stir together cucumber, jicama, and cilantro. Spoon about $^2/_3$ cup of the beef mixture onto each tortilla. Top each with about 2$^1/_2$ tablespoons cucumber mixture and, if desired, sour cream and/or guacamole.
PER SERVING: 369 cal., 9 g total fat (2 g sat. fat), 33 mg chol., 681 mg sodium, 48 g carb., 6 g fiber, 26 g pro. Exchanges: 1 vegetable, 2.5 starch, 2.5 lean meat, 0.5 fat. Carb choices: 3.

A flash in a hot oven helps soften tortillas, making them easier to work with and tastier to eat. To warm tortillas, wrap them in foil and heat in a 350°F oven about 10 minutes.

Here's a full-meal deal—saucy beef, bean, and corn filling crowned with saladlike toppers of cool cucumber and crunchy jicama.

Shredded Beef, Bean, and Corn Fajitas

Ropa Vieja

later

Ropa Vieja

Fire up the flavor of this Cuban-style dish by using the jalapeño pepper.

SERVINGS 6 (about 1 cup beef mixture and ⅓ cup rice each)

CARB. PER SERVING 25 g

- 1 large onion, cut into thin wedges
- 1 medium green sweet pepper, cut into thin strips
- 1 medium red sweet pepper, cut into thin strips
- 3 cloves garlic, minced
- 1 tablespoon cooking oil
- 2 cups Shredded Beef Master Recipe (page 52)
- 1 14.5-ounce can no-salt-added diced tomatoes
- 1 fresh jalapeño chile pepper, seeded and finely chopped* (optional)
- 1 tablespoon red wine vinegar
- 1 teaspoon ground cumin
- ¼ teaspoon black pepper
- 2 cups hot cooked brown rice
- Fresh jalapeño chile pepper slices (optional)

1. In a large skillet, cook onion, sweet peppers, and garlic in hot oil over medium-high heat about 5 minutes or until crisp-tender. Add shredded beef, undrained tomatoes, chopped jalapeño pepper (if using), vinegar, cumin, and black pepper. Bring to boiling; reduce heat. Simmer, uncovered, about 5 minutes or until heated through. Serve over rice. If desired, serve with jalapeño pepper slices.

TEST KITCHEN TIP: Because hot chile peppers contain volatile oils that can burn your skin and eyes, avoid direct contact with chiles as much as possible. When working with chiles, wear plastic or rubber gloves. If your bare hands do touch the chiles, wash your hands well with soap and water.

PER SERVING: 238 cal., 6 g total fat (2 g sat. fat), 33 mg chol., 132 mg sodium, 25 g carb., 4 g fiber, 20 g pro. Exchanges: 1 vegetable, 1 starch, 3 lean meat, 1 fat. Carb choices: 1.5.

later

Philly Shredded Beef Sandwiches

A round loaf of sourdough bread yields large slices that can easily be halved. If baguette-style is all you can find, use eight slices instead of four.

SERVINGS 4 (1 sandwich each)
CARB. PER SERVING 37 g

- 1 large onion, cut into thin wedges
- 2 cloves garlic, minced
- 2 teaspoons olive oil
- 2 cups Shredded Beef Master Recipe (page 52)
- ⅓ cup lower-sodium beef broth
- 3 bottled pepperoncini salad peppers, stems removed and thinly sliced
- 1 teaspoon dried oregano, crushed
- 1 teaspoon paprika
- ½ teaspoon black pepper
- ¼ teaspoon celery seeds
- 4 slices reduced-fat Monterey Jack cheese
- 4 large slices sourdough bread, halved and toasted
- 2 tablespoons light mayonnaise

1. In a large skillet, cook onion and garlic in hot oil over medium heat about 5 minutes or until tender. Add shredded beef, broth, pepperoncini peppers, oregano, paprika, black pepper, and celery seeds. Bring to boiling; reduce heat. Simmer, uncovered, about 5 minutes or until heated through and liquid nearly evaporates.

2. Spoon beef mixture over half of the bread slices. Arrange cheese slices over beef. Spread mayonnaise on remaining bread slices; place, mayonnaise sides down, on top of cheese.

PER SERVING: 454 cal., 17 g total fat (6 g sat. fat), 73 mg chol., 975 mg sodium, 37 g carb., 3 g fiber, 39 g pro. Exchanges: 2.5 starch, 4 lean meat, 1.5 fat. Carb choices: 2.5.

later

Southwestern Shredded Beef Sandwiches

Once you sink your teeth into this yummy stack, you may just lasso it in as one of your favorites.

SERVINGS 4 (1 sandwich each)
CARB. PER SERVING 32 g

- 1 large onion, chopped (1 cup)
- 1 tablespoon cooking oil
- 2 cups Shredded Beef Master Recipe (page 52)
- 1 10-ounce can diced tomatoes and green chiles
- 1 teaspoon ground cumin
- 1 teaspoon chili powder
- 1 tablespoon snipped fresh cilantro
- ½ cup shredded reduced-fat cheddar or Monterey Jack cheese (2 ounces)
- 4 whole wheat hamburger buns, split and toasted
- 1 cup shredded lettuce

1. In a large saucepan, cook onion in hot oil over medium heat about 4 minutes or until tender. Add shredded beef, undrained tomatoes, cumin, and chili powder. Bring to boiling; reduce heat. Simmer, uncovered, about 5 minutes or until heated through and desired consistency. Stir in cilantro.

2. To serve, sprinkle some of the cheese over bottoms of buns. Spoon about ½ cup beef mixture over cheese on each bun. Sprinkle with remaining cheese and the shredded lettuce. Add bun tops.

PER SERVING: 382 cal., 12 g total fat (4 g sat. fat), 58 mg chol., 779 mg sodium, 32 g carb., 4 g fiber, 35 g pro. Exchanges: 1 vegetable, 1.5 starch, 4 lean meat, 1 fat. Carb choices: 2.

Philly Shredded Beef Sandwiches

quick and easy entrées

Thyme-Garlic
Chicken Breasts

Wholesome ingredients lend themselves well to the simple preparation that goes hand in hand with using the slow cooker. Just choose one of these delectable recipes, plan ahead, fill the cooker, and you'll lift the lid on a healthful meal that's ready when you are.

Thyme-Garlic Chicken Breasts

If you grow your own salad greens, use 8 to 9 cups of your favorite combination—baby red or green leaf lettuce, spinach, endive, arugula, mizuna, and more.

SERVINGS 6 to 8
CARB. PER SERVING 10 g

3	to 4 pounds chicken breast halves with bone, skinned
6	cloves garlic, minced
1½	teaspoons dried thyme, crushed
¼	teaspoon salt
¼	cup orange juice
1	tablespoon balsamic vinegar
1	8- to 10-ounce package mixed salad greens
½	cup cherry tomatoes, halved or quartered
¼	cup pitted kalamata olives, halved
¼	cup crumbled reduced-fat feta cheese (1 ounce)
½	cup bottled low-carb vinaigrette salad dressing

1. Sprinkle chicken with garlic, thyme, and salt. Place chicken in a 3½- or 4-quart slow cooker. Pour orange juice and vinegar over chicken.
2. Cover and cook on low-heat setting for 6 to 7 hours or on high-heat setting for 3 to 3½ hours. Remove chicken from slow cooker; cover to keep warm. Discard cooking liquid.
3. In a large bowl, toss together greens, tomatoes, olives, and feta cheese; divide among serving plates. Slice chicken from the bones, discarding bones. Top each salad with some of the chicken. Drizzle dressing over salads.

PER SERVING: 251 cal., 7 g total fat (1 g sat. fat), 87 mg chol., 422 mg sodium, 10 g carb., 1 g fiber, 36 g pro. Exchanges: 1 vegetable, 0.5 starch, 4.5 very lean meat, 0.5 fat. Carb choices: 0.5.

If you can afford some extra carbohydrates, serve this pizza-flavor dish over hot cooked pasta.

Chicken and Pepperoni

Cheesy Garlic Chicken

Two doses of cheese—luscious cream cheese and oozy melted mozzarella—bring extra richness to this dish. Four cloves of garlic make the flavor really soar.

SERVINGS 6 (1 cup each)
CARB. PER SERVING 10 g

- 2 pounds skinless, boneless chicken breast halves, cut into 1½-inch pieces
- 1½ cups cauliflower florets
- 4 cloves garlic, minced
- ¾ cup reduced-sodium chicken broth
- 2 tablespoons quick-cooking tapioca
- ¼ teaspoon salt
- 1½ cups frozen cut green beans
- ½ of an 8-ounce package reduced-fat cream cheese (Neufchâtel), cubed
- ½ cup shredded part-skim mozzarella cheese (2 ounces)
- ⅔ cup chopped roma tomatoes (medium)

1. In a 3½- or 4-quart slow cooker, combine chicken, cauliflower, garlic, broth, tapioca, and salt.
2. Cover and cook on low-heat setting for 3½ to 4½ hours or on high-heat setting for 1½ to 2 hours.
3. If using low-heat setting, turn to high-heat setting. Add beans to mixture in cooker. Cook for 30 minutes more. Turn off cooker.
4. Stir cream cheese into mixture in cooker. Cover and let stand for 10 minutes. Remove cover and gently stir until cream cheese melts and sauce is smooth. Sprinkle each serving with mozzarella cheese and tomatoes.
PER SERVING: 283 cal., 8 g total fat (4 g sat. fat), 108 mg chol., 393 mg sodium, 10 g carb., 2 g fiber, 41 g pro. Exchanges: 0.5 vegetable, 0.5 carb., 5.5 very lean meat, 1 fat. Carb choices: 0.5.

Chicken and Pepperoni

Craving pizza but don't want to order takeout? This dish brings pizza's zesty flavors—pepperoni, olives, an herby tomato sauce, and mozzarella cheese— to a family-friendly chicken supper.

SERVINGS 6
CARB. PER SERVING 1 g

- 3½ to 4 pounds meaty chicken pieces (breast halves, thighs, and drumsticks), skinned
- ⅛ teaspoon salt
- ⅛ teaspoon black pepper
- 2 ounces sliced turkey pepperoni
- ¼ cup sliced pitted ripe olives
- ½ cup reduced-sodium chicken broth
- 1 tablespoon tomato paste
- 1 teaspoon dried Italian seasoning, crushed
- ½ cup shredded part-skim mozzarella cheese (2 ounces)

1. Place chicken in a 3½- to 5-quart slow cooker. Sprinkle chicken with salt and pepper. Cut pepperoni slices in half. Add pepperoni and olives to cooker. In a small bowl, whisk together chicken broth, tomato paste, and Italian seasoning. Add to mixture in cooker.
2. Cover and cook on low-heat setting for 6 to 7 hours or on high-heat setting for 3 to 3½ hours.
3. Using a slotted spoon, transfer chicken, pepperoni, and olives to a serving platter. Discard cooking liquid. Sprinkle chicken with cheese. Cover loosely with foil and let stand for 5 minutes to melt cheese.
PER SERVING: 209 cal., 7 g total fat (2 g sat. fat), 105 mg chol., 484 mg sodium, 1 g carb., 0 g fiber, 33 g pro. Exchanges: 4 lean meat. Carb choices: 0.

Easy Italian Chicken

*This delicious dish goes together
in just 15 minutes.*

SERVINGS 4 to 6
CARB. PER SERVING 21 g

½   of a medium head cabbage, cut into wedges (about
     12 ounces)
1   large onion, sliced and separated into rings
4   to 6 small chicken breast halves (2 to 2½ pounds total),
     skinned
½   teaspoon dried Italian seasoning, crushed
2   cups purchased light spaghetti sauce
2   tablespoons cornstarch
2   tablespoons cold water
     Grated Parmesan cheese (optional)

1. In a 4½- to 6-quart slow cooker, place cabbage and
onion. Add chicken. Sprinkle with Italian seasoning.
Pour spaghetti sauce over all in cooker.
2. Cover and cook on low-heat setting for 4 to 5 hours or
on high-heat setting for 2 to 2½ hours.
3. Transfer chicken to a serving platter, reserving sauce;
cover to keep warm. If using low-heat setting, turn to
high-heat setting. In a small bowl, combine cornstarch
and the water; stir into sauce in cooker. Cover and cook
about 15 minutes more or until thickened. Spoon sauce
over chicken. If desired, sprinkle with Parmesan cheese.
PER SERVING: 259 cal., 2 g total fat (0 g sat. fat), 85 mg chol.,
524 mg sodium, 21 g carb., 6 g fiber, 38 g pro. Exchanges:
1 vegetable, 1 starch, 4.5 very lean meat. Carb
choices: 1.5.

Lemon-Lime Chili Chicken

*Lemon and lime juices add fresh flavor and make
the chicken in this dish ultratender.*

SERVINGS 6 to 8
CARB. PER SERVING 6 g

2   tablespoons chili powder
1   teaspoon salt
½   teaspoon black pepper
3   to 3½ pounds meaty chicken pieces (breast halves,
     thighs, and drumsticks), skinned
1   medium zucchini or yellow summer squash, halved
     lengthwise and cut into 1-inch pieces
1   medium onion, cut into wedges
¼   cup reduced-sodium chicken broth
¼   cup lime juice
¼   cup lemon juice
2   cloves garlic, minced

1. In a small bowl, combine chili powder, salt, and
pepper. Sprinkle spice mixture onto all sides of chicken;
rub in with your fingers. Place chicken in a 4- to 5-quart
slow cooker. Place zucchini and onion on chicken. In a
small bowl, combine broth, lime juice, lemon juice, and
garlic; pour over all in cooker.
2. Cover and cook on low-heat setting for 5 to 6 hours or
on high-heat setting for 2½ to 3 hours.
3. Transfer chicken and vegetables to a serving platter.
Discard cooking liquid.
PER SERVING: 156 cal., 4 g total fat (1 g sat. fat), 76 mg chol.,
525 mg sodium, 6 g carb., 1 g fiber, 24 g pro. Exchanges:
0.5 vegetable, 3 lean meat. Carb choices: 0.5.

Easy Chicken Tetrazzini

Here's a winner—wonderfully homey, crowd-pleasing fare!

SERVINGS 10 (about 1 cup each)
CARB. PER SERVING 25 g

2½   pounds skinless, boneless chicken breast halves and/or
      thighs, cut into 1-inch pieces
2   4.5-ounce jars (drained weight) sliced mushrooms,
      drained
1½   10-ounce cartons refrigerated light Alfredo pasta sauce
¼   cup reduced-sodium chicken broth or water
2   tablespoons dry sherry (optional)
¼   teaspoon ground nutmeg
10   ounces dried multigrain spaghetti
⅔   cup grated Parmesan cheese (3 ounces)
6   green onions, thinly sliced (¾ cup)

1. In a 3½- or 4-quart slow cooker, combine chicken
and mushrooms. In a medium bowl, combine Alfredo
sauce, broth, sherry (if desired), nutmeg, and
¼ teaspoon *black pepper*; pour over all in cooker.
2. Cover and cook on low-heat setting for 5 to 6 hours or
on high-heat setting for 2½ to 3 hours.
3. Meanwhile, cook spaghetti according to package
directions; drain. Stir Parmesan cheese into chicken
mixture in cooker. Serve chicken mixture over
spaghetti; top each serving with green onions.
PER SERVING: 320 cal., 8 g total fat, (4 g sat. fat), 81 mg chol.,
536 mg sodium, 25 g carb., 3 g fiber, 37 g pro. Exchanges:
1.5 starch, 4.5 very lean meat, 0.5 fat. Carb choices: 1.5.

Simple Hoisin Chicken

Hoisin sauce is thick and dark. Slow cooking gives the chicken plenty of time to absorb the sauce's sweet and spicy flavors.

SERVINGS 6
CARB. PER SERVING 31 g

Nonstick cooking spray
12 chicken thighs (3½ to 4 pounds), skinned
2 tablespoons quick-cooking tapioca
⅛ teaspoon salt
⅛ teaspoon black pepper
½ cup bottled hoisin sauce
1 16-ounce package frozen broccoli stir-fry vegetable blend
2 cups hot cooked brown rice

1. Coat a 3½- or 4-quart slow cooker with cooking spray. Place chicken in cooker. Sprinkle chicken with tapioca, salt, and pepper. Top with hoisin sauce.
2. Cover and cook on low-heat setting for 4 to 5 hours or on high-heat setting for 2 to 2½ hours.
3. If using low-heat setting, turn to high-heat setting. Stir in vegetables; cover and cook for 30 to 45 minutes. more. Serve over hot cooked rice.
PER SERVING: 332 cal., 7 g total fat (2 g sat. fat), 126 mg chol., 524 mg sodium, 31 g carb., 3 g fiber, 34 g pro. Exchanges: 1 vegetable, 1.5 starch, 4 very lean meat, 0.5 fat. Carb choices: 2.

Ginger-Tomato Chicken

Keep fresh ginger in a resealable freezer bag in the freezer. It doesn't need to be thawed before use; simply grate what you need and return it to the freezer.

SERVINGS 6 (2 chicken pieces and ⅔ cup sauce each)
CARB. PER SERVING 11 g

12 chicken drumsticks and/or thighs (2½ to 3 pounds), skinned
2 14.5-ounce cans diced tomatoes, drained
2 tablespoons quick-cooking tapioca
1 tablespoon grated fresh ginger or 1 teaspoon ground ginger
1 tablespoon snipped fresh cilantro or parsley
4 cloves garlic, minced
½ teaspoon crushed red pepper
¼ teaspoon salt

1. Place chicken pieces in a 3½- or 4-quart slow cooker. In a medium bowl, combine drained tomatoes, tapioca, ginger, cilantro, garlic, crushed red pepper, and salt. Pour over chicken in cooker.
2. Cover and cook on low-heat setting for 6 to 7 hours or on high-heat setting for 3 to 3½ hours. Skim fat from sauce. Serve sauce with chicken.
PER SERVING: 171 cal., 4 g total fat (1 g sat. fat), 81 mg chol., 444 mg sodium, 11 g carb., 2 g fiber, 23 g pro. Exchanges: 0.5 vegetable, 0.5 starch, 3 lean meat. Carb choices: 1.

Italian Pot Roast

Licoricelike fennel adds a delicate flavor and touch of the Mediterranean to this roast.

SERVINGS 8
CARB. PER SERVING 32 g

1 2½-pound boneless beef chuck pot roast
1 teaspoon fennel seeds, toasted and crushed
½ teaspoon garlic powder
½ teaspoon black pepper
2 medium fennel bulbs, trimmed, cored, and cut into thin wedges
3 medium carrots, halved lengthwise and bias-sliced into 2-inch pieces
1 large onion, cut into thin wedges
1 26-ounce jar light tomato basil pasta sauce
4 cups hot cooked penne pasta
¼ cup snipped fresh Italian (flat-leaf) parsley

1. Trim fat from roast. In a small bowl, combine fennel sees, garlic powder, and pepper. Sprinkle onto roast on all sides; rub in with your fingers. In a 4- to 5-quart slow cooker, combine fennel, carrots, and onion. Place roast on top, cutting roast to fit if necessary. Pour pasta sauce over all in cooker.
2. Cover and cook on low-heat setting for 9 to 10 hours or on high-heat setting for 4½ to 5 hours. Remove roast from cooker; cut into serving-size pieces. Using a slotted spoon, remove vegetables to serve alongside roast. Remove sauce and skim off fat; set aside.
3. Toss hot cooked pasta with parsley. Serve roast, vegetable mixture, and sauce with pasta mixture.
PER SERVING: 341 cal., 7 g total fat (2 g sat. fat), 62 mg chol., 427 mg sodium, 32 g carb., 5 g fiber, 37 g pro. Exchanges: 1 vegetable, 1.5 starch, 4 lean meat, 0.5 fat. Carb choices: 2

Cooked to tender perfection, this roast beef is easier to "pull" into serving-size pieces than to cut. Simply use two forks to pull the meat into the size pieces you want.

Italian Pot Roast

Saucy Beef and Potatoes

Pot Roast with Chipotle-Fruit Sauce

Sweet fruit and smoky chipotle peppers combine in an especially appealing sauce.

SERVINGS 8

CARB. PER SERVING 17 g

- 1 2½- to 3-pound boneless beef chuck pot roast
- 2 teaspoons garlic-pepper seasoning
- 1 7-ounce package dried mixed fruit
- ½ cup water
- 1 tablespoon finely chopped canned chipotle peppers in adobo sauce
- 1 tablespoon cold water
- 2 teaspoons cornstarch

1. Trim fat from roast. Sprinkle both sides of roast with garlic-pepper seasoning. Place roast in 3½- or 4-quart slow cooker, cutting to fit if necessary. Add fruit, the water, and chipotle peppers.

2. Cover and cook on low-heat setting for 10 to 11 hours or on high-heat setting for 5 to 5½ hours.

3. Transfer roast and fruit to a serving platter. Cover to keep warm. Transfer cooking liquid to a bowl; skim off fat. In a medium saucepan, combine the 1 tablespoon cold water and cornstarch; add cooking liquid. Cook and stir until thickened and bubbly; cook and stir for 2 minutes more. Thinly slice roast. To serve, spoon sauce over sliced meat and fruit.

PER SERVING: 251 cal., 6 g total fat (2 g sat. fat), 62 mg chol., 189 mg sodium, 17 g carb., 1 g fiber, 32 g pro. Exchanges: 1 fruit, 4.5 lean meat. Carb choices: 1.

Saucy Beef and Potatoes

Hoisin sauce and salsa sound like an odd couple to season pot roast, but they harmonize perfectly in this meat-and-potato main dish.

SERVINGS 8

CARB. PER SERVING 28 g

- 1 pound baking potatoes, peeled and cut into 1-inch cubes
- 1 pound sweet potatoes, peeled and cut into 1-inch cubes
- 1 2½- to 3-pound fresh beef brisket, fat trimmed
- ½ cup bottled hoisin sauce
- ½ cup bottled salsa
- 2 tablespoons quick-cooking tapioca
- 2 cloves garlic, minced

1. Place baking potatoes and sweet potatoes in a 5- to 6-quart slow cooker. Top with beef brisket. In a small bowl, combine hoisin sauce, salsa, tapioca, and garlic. Pour sauce mixture over brisket; spread evenly.

2. Cover and cook on low-heat setting for 10 to 11 hours or on high-heat setting for 5 to 5½ hours. Transfer meat to a cutting board. Slice across the grain. Serve potatoes and cooking liquid with beef.

PER SERVING: 306 cal., 6 g total fat (2 g sat. fat), 59 mg chol., 484 mg sodium, 28 g carb., 3 g fiber, 33 g pro. Exchanges: 2 starch, 4 lean meat. Carb choices: 2.

Italian Round Steak Dinner

Browning the steak pieces adds a step and a few minutes of prep time but yields appetizing color and richer flavor.

SERVINGS 8

CARB. PER SERVING 33 g

2¼ pounds boneless beef round steak
¼ teaspoon salt
¼ teaspoon black pepper
1 tablespoon cooking oil
1 large fennel bulb, cut into thin wedges
1 large onion, halved and thinly sliced
1 cup packaged fresh julienned carrots
1 28-ounce can crushed tomatoes, undrained
1 15-ounce can no-salt-added tomato sauce
½ cup lower-sodium beef broth
2 teaspoons dried Italian seasoning, crushed
⅛ teaspoon crushed red pepper
3 cups hot cooked multigrain pasta
¼ cup finely shredded Parmesan cheese (1 ounce)

1. Cut steak into eight serving-size pieces; sprinkle with salt and pepper. In a large skillet, brown steak, half at a time, in hot oil over medium-high heat.

2. In a 4- or 4½-quart slow cooker, place fennel, onion, and carrots. Place beef on top of vegetables. In a large bowl, combine tomatoes, tomato sauce, broth, Italian seasoning, and crushed red pepper. Pour over all.

3. Cover and cook on low-heat setting for 9 to 10 hours or on high-heat setting for 4½ to 5 hours.

4. Divide pasta among eight serving plates; top each with a steak portion and sauce. Sprinkle with cheese.

PER SERVING: 365 cal., 8 g total fat (2 g sat. fat), 72 mg chol., 535 mg sodium, 33 g carb., 6 g fiber, 36 g pro. Exchanges: 1 vegetable, 2 starch, 4 lean meat. Carb choices: 2.

Southwestern Steak Roll-Ups

Flank steak, peppers, onions, and tomatoes spiked with chili powder simmer into a stew that tastes great wrapped in a warmed tortilla.

SERVINGS 6 (1 tortilla and about 1 cup meat and vegetables each)

CARB. PER SERVING 23 g

1½ pounds beef flank steak
1 16-ounce package frozen stir-fry vegetables (green, red, and yellow peppers and onions)
1 14.5-ounce can Mexican-style stewed tomatoes, undrained
1 small fresh jalapeño chile pepper, seeded and finely chopped* (optional)
2 teaspoons chili powder
6 6- to 7-inch white or whole wheat flour tortillas, warmed**
 Lime wedges (optional)

1. Place steak in a 3½- or 4-quart slow cooker, cutting to fit if necessary. Add frozen vegetables. In a medium bowl, stir together undrained tomatoes, jalapeño pepper (if using), and chili powder. Pour over all in cooker.

2. Cover and cook on low-heat setting for 7 to 8 hours or on high-heat setting for 3½ to 4 hours. Remove meat from cooker; slice across the grain. Using a slotted spoon, remove vegetables from cooker. Divide meat and vegetables among warm tortillas; roll up. If desired, serve with lime wedges.

*TEST KITCHEN TIP: Because hot chile peppers contain volatile oils that can burn your skin and eyes, avoid direct contact with chiles as much as possible. When working with chiles, wear plastic or rubber gloves. If your bare hands do touch chiles, wash your hands well with soap and water.

**TEST KITCHEN TIP: To warm tortillas, wrap tightly in foil. Heat in a 350°F oven about 10 minutes or until heated through.

PER SERVING: 315 cal., 10 g total fat (2 g sat. fat), 37 mg chol., 326 mg sodium, 23 g carb., 1 g fiber, 29 g pro. Exchanges: 1.5 vegetable, 1 starch, 3 lean meat, 1 fat. Carb choices: 1.5.

Southwestern
Steak Roll-Ups

Shredded Pork Salad

Shredded meat is a welcome change from sliced roast.
This slow-cooker method makes it especially tender.

SERVINGS 6 (2 lettuce leaves, ½ cup meat,
and 2 tablespoons salsa each)

CARB. PER SERVING 10 g

1. Trim fat from meat. If necessary, cut meat to fit in a 3½- or 4-quart slow cooker. Place meat in the cooker. Add the water, onions, jalapeño peppers, garlic, coriander, cumin, oregano, salt, and black pepper.
2. Cover and cook on low-heat setting for 8 to 10 hours or on high-heat setting for 4 to 5 hours.
3. Remove meat from cooker; discard cooking liquid. Using two forks, shred meat. To serve, spoon warm meat on lettuce leaves. Top with salsa. If desired, garnish with *fresh oregano*.

1	2-pound boneless pork shoulder roast
1	cup water
2	large onions, quartered
3	fresh jalapeño chile peppers, cut up*
8	cloves garlic, minced
2	teaspoons ground coriander
2	teaspoons ground cumin
2	teaspoons dried oregano, crushed
½	teaspoon salt
½	teaspoon black pepper
12	Bibb lettuce leaves
¾	cup purchased fresh salsa or bottled salsa

*TEST KITCHEN TIP: Because hot chile peppers contain volatile oils that can burn your skin and eyes, avoid direct contact with chiles as much as possible. When working with chiles, wear plastic or rubber gloves. If your bare hands do touch the chiles, wash your hands well with soap and water.

PER SERVING: 278 cal., 12 g total fat (4 g sat. fat), 102 mg chol., 402 mg sodium, 10 g carb., 3 g fiber, 32 g pro. Exchanges: 1.5 vegetable, 4 lean meat, 1.5 fat. Carb choices: 0.5.

Herbed Pork

You'll want to serve this herb-rubbed pork roast with a colorful vegetable side dish or salad.

SERVINGS 10

CARB. PER SERVING 1 g

- 1 3½- to 4-pound boneless pork shoulder roast
- 2 teaspoons fennel seeds, crushed
- 1 teaspoon ground sage
- 1 teaspoon dried marjoram, crushed
- 1 teaspoon celery seeds, crushed
- 1 teaspoon dry mustard
- ¼ teaspoon salt
- ¼ teaspoon black pepper
- ¾ cup light beer or water

1. Trim fat from roast. If necessary, cut roast to fit in a 3½- or 4-quart slow cooker. In a small bowl, combine fennel seeds, sage, marjoram, celery seeds, mustard, salt, and pepper. Sprinkle fennel mixture evenly over roast; rub in with your fingers. Place roast in cooker. Pour beer over roast.

2. Cover and cook on low-heat setting for 8 to 10 hours or on high-heat setting for 4 to 5 hours. Transfer meat to a serving platter; discard cooking liquid.

PER SERVING: 227 cal., 9 g total fat (3 g sat. fat), 103 mg chol., 190 mg sodium, 1 g carb., 0 g fiber, 32 g pro. Exchanges: 4 lean meat. Carb choices: 0.

Braised Pork with Salsa Verde

Because it starts with a jar of salsa verde, the sauce is green and fresh-tasting.

SERVINGS 6 (1 cup pork mixture and ½ cup rice each)

CARB. PER SERVING 31 g

- 1 large onion, cut into thin wedges
- 1½ pounds boneless pork loin, cut into 1½-inch pieces
- 2 large tomatoes, coarsely chopped (1⅓ cups)
- 1 16-ounce jar green salsa (salsa verde)
- ½ cup reduced-sodium chicken broth
- 2 cloves garlic, minced
- 1 teaspoon ground cumin
- ¼ teaspoon black pepper
- 3 cups hot cooked brown rice
- Snipped fresh cilantro

1. In a 3½- or 4-quart slow cooker, place onion and pork. Top with tomatoes, salsa, chicken broth, garlic, cumin, and pepper.

2. Cover and cook on low-heat setting for 6 to 6½ hours or on high-heat setting for 3 hours. Serve with hot cooked brown rice and top each serving with cilantro.

PER SERVING: 297 cal., 6 g total fat (1 g sat. fat), 78 mg chol., 231 mg sodium, 31 g carb., 3 g fiber, 29 g pro. Exchanges: 0.5 vegetable, 2 starch, 3 lean meat. Carb choices: 2.

Sassy Pork Chops

The sass in these chops comes from the perfect blend of chipotle chile peppers—they really spice up this dish! Note: Freeze leftover chipotle peppers, covered in some of the adobo sauce, in a tightly sealed freezer container.

SERVINGS 8

CARB. PER SERVING 4 g

- 2 medium red, green, and/or yellow sweet peppers, cut into strips
- 2 stalks celery, thinly sliced (1 cup)
- 1 medium onion, chopped (½ cup)
- 8 pork loin chops (with bone), cut ¾ inch thick
- ½ teaspoon garlic salt
- ¼ teaspoon black pepper
- 2 tablespoons cooking oil
- ¼ cup reduced-sodium chicken broth
- ¼ cup orange juice
- 1 tablespoon chopped chipotle chile peppers in adobo sauce
- ½ teaspoon dried oregano, crushed

1. In a 4- to 5-quart slow cooker, place sweet peppers, celery, and onion; set aside. Season chops with garlic salt and black pepper. In a 12-inch skillet, cook chops, half at a time, in hot oil over medium heat until browned on both sides. Add chops to cooker. In a small bowl, combine broth, orange juice, chipotle peppers, and oregano. Pour over all in cooker.

2. Cover and cook on low-heat setting for 6 to 7 hours or on high-heat setting for 3 to 3½ hours. Using a slotted spoon, transfer chops and vegetables to a serving platter; discard cooking liquid.

PER SERVING: 215 cal., 7 g total fat (1 g sat. fat), 78 mg chol., 363 mg sodium, 4 g carb., 1 g fiber, 33 g pro. Exchanges: 1 vegetable, 4 lean meat. Carb choices: 0.

Creamy Veggies, Tofu, and Pasta

Tofu provides the protein for this one-dish meal. It's a great way to add soy to your diet.

SERVINGS 8 (about 1⅓ cups each)
CARB. PER SERVING 32 g

- 2 14.5-ounce cans no-salt-added diced tomatoes, undrained
- 1 10.75-ounce can reduced-fat and reduced-sodium condensed cream of mushroom soup
- 4 medium carrots, sliced (2 cups)
- 3 stalks celery, sliced (1½ cups)
- 3 medium onions, chopped (1½ cups)
- 4 cloves garlic, minced
- 2 teaspoons dried Italian seasoning, crushed
- ½ teaspoon salt
- ¼ teaspoon black pepper
- 1 16- to 18-ounce package tub-style extra-firm tofu (fresh bean curd), drained and cubed
- 8 ounces dried multigrain spaghetti, broken and cooked according to package directions
- ½ cup shredded reduced-fat cheddar cheese (2 ounces)

1. In a 3½- or 4-quart slow cooker, stir together the undrained tomatoes and soup. Stir in the carrots, celery, onions, garlic, Italian seasoning, salt, and pepper.
2. Cover and cook on low-heat setting for 7 to 8 hours or on high-heat setting for 3½ to 4 hours.
3. Gently stir in tofu cubes and cooked spaghetti. Sprinkle each serving with cheese.
PER SERVING: 212 cal., 4 g total fat (1 g sat. fat), 5 mg chol., 464 mg sodium, 32 g carb., 5 g fiber, 13 g pro. Exchanges: 1.5 vegetable, 1.5 starch, 1 lean meat. Carb choices: 2.

Sweet Beans and Lentils over Polenta

Look for tubes of refrigerated polenta in the produce section of the supermarket. The varieties seasoned with wild mushrooms or Italian herbs are especially tasty in this dish.

SERVINGS 6 (1 cup lentil mixture and ½ cup polenta each)
CARB. PER SERVING 43 g

- 1 14-ounce can vegetable broth
- 1 12-ounce package frozen shelled sweet soybeans (edamame)
- 1 cup dry brown lentils, rinsed and drained
- 1 medium red sweet pepper, chopped (¾ cup)
- ½ cup water
- 1 teaspoon dried oregano, crushed
- 2 cloves garlic, minced
- 1 16-ounce tube refrigerated polenta
- 2 medium tomatoes, chopped (1 cup)

1. In a 3½- or 4-quart slow cooker, combine broth, soybeans, lentils, sweet pepper, the water, oregano, and garlic.
2. Cover and cook on low-heat setting for 7 to 8 hours or on high-heat setting for 3½ to 4 hours.
3. Prepare polenta according to package directions. Stir tomatoes into lentil mixture; serve over polenta.
PER SERVING: 279 cal., 4 g total fat (0 g sat. fat), 0 mg chol., 580 mg sodium, 43 g carb., 15 g fiber, 18 g pro. Exchanges: 1 vegetable, 2.5 starch, 1.5 very lean meat. Carb choices: 3.

Chili Bean-Stuffed Peppers

This meatless main dish goes together in a jiffy. Choose any color of sweet pepper; they're equally high in vitamin C.

SERVINGS 4
CARB. PER SERVING 49 g

- 4 small to medium green, red, or yellow sweet peppers
- 1 cup cooked converted rice
- 1 15-ounce can chili beans with chili gravy
- 1 15-ounce can or two 8-ounce cans no-salt-added tomato sauce
- ⅓ cup finely chopped onion
- ¾ cup shredded reduced-fat Monterey Jack cheese (3 ounces)

1. Remove tops, membranes, and seeds from sweet peppers. Chop enough tops to make ⅓ cup; set aside. If necessary, cut a thin slice from the bottom of each pepper so they sit flat. In a medium bowl, stir together rice and undrained beans. Spoon about ¾ cup rice mixture into each pepper. Pour tomato sauce into the bottom of a 4½- to 6-quart slow cooker; stir in reserved chopped peppers and onion. Place peppers, filled sides up, in cooker.
2. Cover and cook on low-heat setting for 6 to 6½ hours or on high-heat setting for 3 to 3½ hours.
3. To serve, transfer peppers to a platter and, if desired, cut in half. Sprinkle cheese over tops of peppers. Serve with tomato sauce.
PER SERVING: 304 cal., 6 g total fat (3 g sat. fat), 15 mg chol., 523 mg sodium, 49 g carb., 10 g fiber, 13 g pro. Exchanges: 1.5 vegetable, 2.5 starch, 0.5 lean meat, 0.5 fat. Carb choices: 3.

A Sweet Deal

Colorful sweet peppers are packed with great flavor as well as a multitude of vitamins and other nutrients. Cooked or eaten raw, they make a tasty treat. Here are some easy ways to introduce this high-fiber veggie into your diet.

1. **Dunk** strips in hummus for a snack.

2. **Toss** bite-size pieces in a green salad.

3. **Add** finely chopped pieces to your prized meat loaf recipe.

4. **Parboil** them whole to fill with your favorite couscous or rice mixture.

5. **Top** a pizza with thinly sliced rings.

7. **Sauté** chopped pieces with other veggies to use as an omelet filling.

8. **Layer** plank-size pieces on a sandwich.

9. **Munch** on them plain when you're craving something crunchy.

10. **Roast** sweet peppers for an extra-flavorful treat.

Chili Bean-Stuffed Peppers

Tiny couscous beads cook in just 5 minutes. Before you dig in to this curry-flavored dish, grab a fork and give it a gentle stir to fluff the couscous.

Curried Couscous with Vegetables

Curried Couscous with Vegetables

This recipe is a hodgepodge of flavor and texture: savory-sweet with zing from the jalapeño pepper and a subtle crunch from the toasted almonds.

SERVINGS 8 (1 cup each)
CARB. PER SERVING 40 g

- 1 large onion, cut into thin wedges
- 2 medium yellow summer squash and/or zucchini, coarsely chopped (2 cups)
- 2 14.5-ounce cans no-salt-added diced tomatoes, undrained
- 2 cups water
- 2 5.7-ounce packages curry-flavor couscous mix
- 1 fresh jalapeño chile pepper, seeded and finely chopped*
- 1 cup slivered almonds, toasted
- ½ cup raisins (optional)
- Cilantro sprigs (optional)

1. In a 3½- or 4-quart slow cooker, combine onion, squash, undrained tomatoes, the water, seasoning packets from couscous mixes, and the jalapeño pepper.

2. Cover and cook on low-heat setting for 4 to 6 hours or on high-heat setting for 2 to 3 hours. Stir in couscous. Turn off cooker. Cover and let stand for 5 minutes. Fluff couscous mixture with a fork.

3. To serve, sprinkle each serving with almonds and, if desired, raisins. If desired, garnish with cilantro sprigs.

*TEST KITCHEN TIP: Because hot chile peppers contain volatile oils that can burn your skin and eyes, avoid direct contact with chiles as much as possible. When working with chiles, wear plastic or rubber gloves. If your bare hands do touch chiles, wash your hands well with soap and water.

PER SERVING: 248 cal., 7 g total fat (1 g sat. fat), 0 mg chol., 436 mg sodium, 40 g carb., 6 g fiber, 10 g pro. Exchanges: 1 vegetable, 2.5 starch, 1 fat. Carb choices: 2.5.

Lentil and Bulgur Pilaf with Feta

Here's a hearty meatless meal that cooks in 3 hours flat, so you can start it late afternoon and still eat it for supper.

SERVINGS 6 (1⅓ cups each)
CARB. PER SERVING 45 g

- 1 14-ounce can vegetable or chicken broth
- 4 medium carrots, sliced (2 cups)
- 2 cups frozen whole kernel corn
- 1¾ cups water
- 1 cup bulgur
- ½ cup brown lentils, rinsed and drained
- 1 teaspoon dried oregano, crushed
- 1 teaspoon ground cumin
- ¼ teaspoon ground coriander
- ¼ teaspoon black pepper
- 4 cloves garlic, minced
- 4 medium tomatoes, chopped (2 cups)
- ¾ cup crumbled reduced-fat feta cheese (3 ounces)

1. In a 3½- or 4-quart slow cooker, combine broth, carrots, corn, the water, bulgur, lentils, oregano, cumin, coriander, pepper, and garlic. Cover and cook on high-heat setting for 3 hours.

2. Stir in tomatoes. Turn off cooker. Cover and let stand for 10 minutes. Sprinkle each serving with feta cheese.

PER SERVING: 248 cal., 3 g total fat (2 g sat. fat), 5 mg chol., 553 mg sodium, 45 g carb., 12 g fiber, 13 g pro. Exchanges: 1 vegetable, 2.5 starch, 0.5 very lean meat. Carb choices: 3.

global
favorites

Mediterranean Beef Ragoût

Some of the most

joyful travel moments

include the journeys

your taste buds take.

Begin a culinary trip

around the world with

these international

favorites designed for

a slow simmer in your

slow cooker. Along the

way, discover how good

for you these delicious

entrées are, too.

Mediterranean Beef Ragoût

Gremolata, a blend of fresh parsley, lemon peel, and garlic, brightens the flavor and appearance of this rich stew.

SERVINGS 6 (1⅓ cups beef mixture and ⅓ cup couscous each)

CARB. PER SERVING 29 g

1½ pounds lean beef stew meat, cut into 1-inch cubes
1 tablespoon olive oil
2 medium onions, cut into thin wedges
3 medium carrots, cut into ½-inch slices (1½ cups)
2 cloves garlic, minced
1 teaspoon dried thyme, crushed
¼ teaspoon salt
¼ teaspoon black pepper
1 14.5-ounce can diced tomatoes, undrained
½ cup lower-sodium beef broth
1 medium zucchini, halved lengthwise and cut into ¼-inch slices
6 ounces fresh green beans, cut into 2-inch pieces
2 cups hot cooked whole wheat couscous or brown rice
Gremolata (below)

1. In a large skillet, brown meat, half at a time, in hot oil over medium-high heat. Drain off fat. Transfer meat to a 3½- or 4-quart slow cooker. Add onions, carrots, garlic, thyme, salt, and pepper. Pour undrained tomatoes and broth over all in cooker.

2. Cover and cook on low-heat setting for 7 to 9 hours or on high-heat setting for 3½ to 4½ hours.

3. If using low-heat setting, turn to high-heat setting. Stir in zucchini and green beans. Cover and cook for 30 minutes more. Serve over hot cooked couscous. Top individual servings with Gremolata.

GREMOLATA: In a small bowl, stir together ¼ cup snipped fresh parsley, 1 tablespoon finely shredded lemon peel, and 2 cloves garlic, minced.

PER SERVING: 329 cal., 11 g total fat (3 g sat. fat), 55 mg chol., 367 mg sodium, 29 g carb., 6 g fiber, 30 g pro. Exchanges: 1.5 vegetable, 1.5 starch, 3 lean meat, 1 fat. Carb choices: 2.

Hungarian Paprikash

Paprikash (PAH-pree-kash) is a Hungarian dish made with meat, onions, and—as its name hints—paprika. This long-braising stew is a natural for the slow cooker.

SERVINGS 8 (about ¾ cup beef mixture and ½ cup noodles each)

CARB. PER SERVING 31 g

2 medium onions, sliced
1 large red or green sweet pepper, chopped (1 cup)
2 pounds lean beef stew meat, cut into 1-inch pieces
1 4.5-ounce jar sliced mushrooms, drained
1 14.5-ounce can diced tomatoes, drained
1 10.75-ounce can condensed reduced-fat, reduced-sodium cream of mushroom soup
1 tablespoon Hungarian paprika or paprika
1 teaspoon dried thyme, crushed
¼ teaspoon coarsely ground black pepper
4 cups hot cooked noodles or spaetzle
½ cup light sour cream

1. In a 3½- or 4-quart slow cooker, place onions and sweet pepper. Add meat and mushrooms.
2. In a medium bowl, stir together drained tomatoes, soup, paprika, thyme, and black pepper. Pour over all in cooker.
3. Cover and cook on low-heat setting for 8 to 10 hours or on high-heat setting for 4 to 5 hours. Serve meat mixture over hot cooked noodles. Top individual servings with sour cream.

PER SERVING: 331 cal., 9 g total fat (3 g sat. fat), 78 mg chol., 400 mg sodium, 31 g carb., 4 g fiber, 31 g pro. Exchanges: 1 vegetable, 1.5 starch, 3.5 lean meat. Carb choices: 2.

Russian Braised Brisket

Adding cabbage, mushrooms, and sauce just before the meat is done ensures that each part of the meal is just the right doneness at serving time.

SERVINGS 6 (4 ounces meat and 1 cup vegetable sauce mixture each)

CARB. PER SERVING 21 g

1 2-pound beef brisket
½ teaspoon salt
¼ teaspoon black pepper
1 tablespoon cooking oil
1 large onion, cut into wedges
2 medium parsnips, cut into 2-inch pieces
2 medium carrots, cut into 2-inch pieces
½ teaspoon dill seeds
½ teaspoon caraway seeds
1½ cups lower-sodium beef broth
¼ cup vodka (optional)
1 8-ounce carton light sour cream
⅓ cup all-purpose flour
¼ cup water
2 teaspoons dried dill weed
2 teaspoons horseradish mustard
2 cups finely shredded cabbage
1 cup sliced fresh mushrooms

1. Trim fat from brisket. Cut brisket to fit in a 3½- or 4-quart slow cooker. Sprinkle brisket with ¼ teaspoon of the salt and the pepper. In a large skillet, brown brisket in hot oil over medium-high heat.
2. In the slow cooker, place onion, parsnips, and carrots. Sprinkle with dill and caraway seeds and the remaining ¼ teaspoon salt. Top with brisket. Pour broth and vodka, if using, over all in cooker.
3. Cover and cook on low-heat setting for 10 hours or on high-heat setting for 5 hours.
4. If using low-heat setting, turn to high-heat setting. In a medium bowl, stir together sour cream, flour, the water, dill weed, and mustard until smooth. Stir about 1 cup of the hot cooking liquid into the sour cream mixture. Return all to cooker; stir to combine. Stir in cabbage and mushrooms. Cover and cook for 30 to 60 minutes more or until vegetables are tender and liquid is thickened and bubbly.
5. Transfer brisket to a cutting board and slice thinly across the grain. Serve with sauce and vegetables.

PER SERVING: 348 cal., 13 g total fat (5 g sat. fat), 75 mg chol., 482 mg sodium, 21 g carb., 4 g fiber, 37 g pro. Exchanges: 1 vegetable, 1 starch, 4.5 lean meat. Carb choices: 1.5.

German-Style Beef Roast

Red wine, chopped dill pickles, and hearty mustard set this succulent beef pot roast apart from the rest.

SERVINGS 8 (about 4 ounces meat, ½ cup spaetzle, and ⅔ cup sauce each)

CARB. PER SERVING 30 g

- 1 2½- to 3-pound boneless beef chuck pot roast
- 2 teaspoons cooking oil
- 4 medium carrots, sliced (2 cups)
- 2 large onions, chopped (2 cups)
- 2 stalks celery, sliced (1 cup)
- ¾ cup chopped kosher-style dill pickles
- ½ cup dry red wine or lower-sodium beef broth
- ⅓ cup German-style mustard
- ½ teaspoon coarsely ground black pepper
- ¼ teaspoon ground cloves
- 2 bay leaves
- 2 tablespoons all-purpose flour
- 2 tablespoons dry red wine or lower-sodium beef broth
- 4 cups hot cooked spaetzle or noodles
  Snipped fresh parsley (optional)

1. Trim fat from roast. If necessary, cut roast to fit in a 3½- or 4-quart slow cooker. In a large nonstick skillet, brown the roast on all sides in hot oil over medium-high heat.

2. Meanwhile, in the cooker, combine carrots, onions, celery, and pickles. Place the meat on the vegetables. In a small bowl, combine the ½ cup red wine, the mustard, pepper, cloves, and bay leaves. Pour over all in cooker.

3. Cover and cook on low-heat setting for 10 to 11 hours or on high-heat setting for 5 to 5½ hours.

4. Transfer meat to a serving platter; cover to keep warm. Transfer vegetables and cooking liquid to a 2-quart saucepan. Skim off fat. Discard bay leaves. In a small bowl, stir together flour and the 2 tablespoons red wine. Stir into mixture in saucepan. Cook and stir over medium heat until thickened and bubbly; cook and stir for 1 minute more. Slice meat. Serve meat and vegetables with sauce and hot cooked spaetzle. If desired, sprinkle with parsley.

PER SERVING: 363 cal., 7 g total fat (2 g sat. fat), 106 mg chol., 704 mg sodium, 30 g carb., 3 g fiber, 36 g pro. Exchanges: 0.5 vegetable, 1.5 starch, 4.5 lean meat, 0.5 fat. Carb choices: 2.

German-Style Beef Roast

Although spaetzle is classic German fare, you can also serve this tangy-sauced beef roast over hot cooked egg noodles or even potato gnocchi.

Beef Fajitas

Beef Fajitas

Shredded carrots and lettuce provide a fresh note to slow-simmered meat and vegetables.

SERVINGS 8 (1 tortilla and ½ cup meat mixture each)

CARB. PER SERVING 20 g

- 1 large onion, cut into thin wedges
- 2 pounds boneless beef sirloin steak
- 1 teaspoon ground cumin
- 1 teaspoon ground coriander
- ½ teaspoon black pepper
- ¼ teaspoon salt
- 2 medium red or green sweet peppers, cut into thin bite-size strips
- ¼ cup lower-sodium beef broth
- 8 7- to 8-inch whole wheat or plain flour tortillas
- 1 cup shredded carrots
- 1 cup coarsely shredded lettuce
- ½ cup bottled salsa (optional)
- ⅓ cup purchased guacamole (optional)
- ⅓ cup light sour cream (optional)

1. Place onion in a 3½- or 4-quart slow cooker. Trim fat from steak. Sprinkle one side of the steak with cumin, coriander, black pepper, and salt; rub in with your fingers. Cut steak across the grain into thin bite-size strips. Add beef strips to cooker. Top with sweet peppers. Pour broth over all in cooker.

2. Cover and cook on low-heat setting for 7 to 8 hours or on high-heat setting for 3½ to 4 hours.

3. To serve, use a slotted spoon to spoon beef-vegetable mixture onto tortillas. Top each serving with carrots and lettuce. Fold tortillas over. If desired, serve with salsa, guacamole, and sour cream.

PER SERVING: 298 cal., 8 g total fat (2 g sat. fat), 68 mg chol., 485 mg sodium, 20 g carb., 12 g fiber, 33 g pro. Exchanges: 0.5 vegetable, 1 starch, 4 lean meat. Carb choices: 1.

Steak with Tuscan Tomato Sauce

A can of diced tomatoes seasoned with garlic and herbs keeps both the ingredients list and prep time short.

SERVINGS 4 (3 ounces meat and about ⅓ cup sauce each)
CARB. PER SERVING 16 g

- 1 pound boneless beef round steak, cut 1 inch thick
- 1 tablespoon cooking oil
- 1 medium onion, sliced
- 2 tablespoons quick-cooking tapioca, crushed
- 1 teaspoon dried thyme, crushed
- ¼ teaspoon black pepper
- 1 14.5-ounce can diced tomatoes with basil, garlic, and oregano, undrained
- 2 cups hot cooked noodles or brown rice (optional)
- Fresh thyme sprigs (optional)

1. Trim fat from steak. In a large skillet, brown steak on both sides in hot oil over medium heat. Drain off fat.
2. Place onion in a 3½- or 4-quart slow cooker. Sprinkle with tapioca, thyme, and pepper. Pour undrained tomatoes over onion in cooker. Place steak on mixture in cooker.
3. Cover and cook on low-heat setting for 8 to 10 hours or on high-heat setting for 4 to 5 hours. Transfer meat to a cutting board. Slice meat; serve with cooking sauce and, if desired, hot cooked noodles. If desired, garnish with fresh thyme.

PER SERVING: 230 cal., 6 g total fat (1 g sat. fat), 49 mg chol., 595 mg sodium, 16 g carb., 1 g fiber, 28 g pro. Exchanges: 1 vegetable, 0.5 starch, 2.5 lean meat. Carb choices: 1.

Italian Steak Rolls

Stuffed with veggies and Parmesan cheese, these beef bundles cook up moist and tender in bottled spaghetti sauce.

SERVINGS 6 (1 steak roll, ½ cup wilted spinach, and about ½ cup sauce each)
CARB. PER SERVING 15 g

- ½ cup shredded carrot
- ⅓ cup chopped zucchini
- ⅓ cup chopped red or green sweet pepper
- 2 green onions, sliced (¼ cup)
- 2 tablespoons grated Parmesan cheese
- 1 tablespoon snipped fresh parsley
- 1 clove garlic, minced
- 6 tenderized beef round steaks (about 2 pounds total)*
- 2 cups meatless spaghetti sauce
- 3 cups wilted spinach or wilted trimmed Swiss chard**

1. In a small bowl, combine carrot, zucchini, sweet pepper, green onions, Parmesan cheese, parsley, garlic, and ¼ teaspoon *black pepper*. Spoon ¼ cup of the vegetable filling onto each piece of meat. Roll up meat around the filling; secure with 100-percent-cotton kitchen string or wooden toothpicks.
2. Place meat rolls in a 3½- or 4-quart slow cooker. Pour spaghetti sauce over the meat rolls.
3. Cover and cook on low-heat setting for 8 to 10 hours or on high-heat setting for 4 to 5 hours. Discard string or toothpicks. Skim fat from sauce and serve with meat rolls and wilted spinach.

*TEST KITCHEN TIP: If you can't find tenderized round steak, ask a butcher to tenderize 2 pounds boneless beef round steak and cut it into six pieces. Or cut 2 pounds boneless beef round steak into six serving-size pieces; place each steak piece between two pieces of plastic wrap. Using a meat mallet, pound the steak pieces until ¼ to ½ inch thick.

**TEST KITCHEN TIP: Place 9 ounces baby spinach (about 9 cups) or 1 pound trimmed and torn Swiss chard in a steamer basket over boiling water. Cover and steam spinach for 2 to 3 minutes or chard about 6 minutes or until wilted.

PER SERVING: 281 cal., 9 g total fat (3 g sat. fat), 73 mg chol., 545 mg sodium, 15 g carb., 4 g fiber, 37 g pro. Exchanges: 1.5 vegetable, 0.5 carb., 4.5 lean meat. Carb choices: 1.

Italian Steak Rolls

Chile Verde

Mexico's famous pork shoulder braise simmers up beautifully in the slow cooker. Serve this colorful dish with a bright, vinaigrette-tossed salad topped with sparkling orange slices.

SERVINGS 6 (2 tortillas and 1 cup pork mixture each)

CARB. PER SERVING 32 g

- 1 teaspoon ground cumin
- ½ teaspoon salt
- ¼ teaspoon black pepper
- 1½ pounds boneless pork shoulder roast
  Nonstick cooking spray
- 1 tablespoon olive oil
- 1 pound fresh tomatillos, husks removed and chopped (about 4 cups)
- 1 large onion, chopped (1 cup)
- 3 teaspoons finely shredded lime peel, divided
- 2 tablespoons lime juice
- 4 cloves garlic, minced
- 1 medium yellow or red sweet pepper, chopped (¾ cup)
- 12 6-inch corn tortillas
- 2 tablespoons snipped fresh cilantro
  Purchased green salsa (optional)
  Lime wedges (optional)

1. In a small bowl, combine cumin, salt, and black pepper; set aside. Trim fat from roast. Cut roast into 1-inch pieces. Sprinkle cumin mixture over meat. Coat a large skillet with cooking spray. In the hot skillet, brown half of the meat over medium heat. Remove meat from skillet. Add oil to skillet. Brown remaining meat in hot oil. Drain off fat.

2. Place meat in a 3½- or 4-quart slow cooker. Add tomatillos, onion, 1 teaspoon of the lime peel, lime juice, and garlic. Stir to combine.

3. Cover and cook on low-heat setting for 6 to 8 hours or on high-heat setting for 3 to 4 hours.

4. If using low-heat setting, turn to high-heat setting. Add sweet pepper to cooker. Cover and cook for 15 minutes more. Fill corn tortillas with meat mixture; sprinkle with cilantro and remaining lime peel. If desired, serve with green salsa and lime wedges.

PER SERVING: 333 cal., 11 g total fat (3 g sat. fat), 73 mg chol., 314 mg sodium, 32 g carb., 4 g fiber, 27 g pro. Exchanges: 1 vegetable, 2 starch, 3 lean meat, 0.5 fat. Carb choices: 2.

Adapt Your Favorites

Try these helpful tips for adapting one of your favorite stove-top recipes to the slow cooker.

1. **Start** with a recipe that calls for a less-tender meat cut.

2. **Find** a recipe in this book that is similar to yours; use it as a guide for quantities, piece sizes, liquid levels, and cooking times.

3. **Cut** vegetables into bite-size pieces; place them at the bottom of the slow cooker so they cook evenly and completely.

4. **Cut** the meat to the right size for the slow cooker and, if desired, brown it before adding to the cooker.

5. **Unless** your dish contains long grain rice, reduce the liquids in the recipe you are adapting by half.

6. **Adjust** cooking time by multiplying your recipe's traditional-method cooking time by 6 for slow cooking on the high-heat setting and by 4 for slow cooking on the low-heat setting.

Chile Verde

Carnitas

With a bouquet garni, removing the seasonings from dishes like this slow-simmered pork is a cinch—there's no fishing around for individual pieces. Just use a slotted spoon to remove the pouch of seasonings from the cooking liquid. If you don't have cheesecloth on hand, substitute a coffee filter.

SERVINGS 6 (2 tortillas and about 1⅓ cups meat mixture each)

CARB. PER SERVING 24 g

2 pounds boneless pork shoulder roast, cut into 2-inch pieces
¼ teaspoon salt
¼ teaspoon black pepper
1 tablespoon whole black peppercorns
2 teaspoons cumin seeds
4 cloves garlic, minced
1 teaspoon dried oregano, crushed
3 bay leaves
2 14-ounce cans reduced-sodium chicken broth
2 teaspoons finely shredded lime peel
2 tablespoons lime juice
12 6-inch crisp corn tortillas
2 green onions, thinly sliced (¼ cup)
⅓ cup light sour cream (optional)
⅓ cup purchased salsa (optional)

1. Sprinkle pork with salt and pepper. Place pork in a 3½- or 4-quart slow cooker.

2. To make a bouquet garni, cut a 6-inch square from a double thickness of 100-percent-cotton cheesecloth. Place peppercorns, cumin seeds, garlic, oregano, and bay leaves in center of cheesecloth square. Gather corners of cheesecloth and tie with 100-percent-cotton kitchen string. Add to slow cooker. Pour broth over all in cooker.

3. Cover and cook on low-heat setting for 10 to 12 hours or on high-heat setting for 4½ to 5 hours.

4. Using a slotted spoon, remove meat from slow cooker. Discard bouquet garni and cooking liquid. Using two forks, coarsely shred meat; discard fat. Sprinkle meat with lime peel and lime juice; toss to mix. Top tortillas with meat mixture. Sprinkle with green onions. If desired, serve with sour cream and salsa.

PER SERVING: 318 cal., 10 g total fat (3 g sat. fat), 90 mg chol., 377 mg sodium, 24 g carb., 4 g fiber, 32 g pro. Exchanges: 1.5 starch, 4 lean meat. Carb choices: 1.5.

Carnitas

Sweet-and-Sour Pork

Skip the traditional last-minute stir-frying and get the same great flavor with this saucy, slow-simmered version.

SERVINGS 8 (1 cup pork mixture and ⅓ cup rice each)

CARB. PER SERVING 41 g

1 20-ounce can pineapple chunks (juice pack)
2 medium carrots, bias-sliced (1 cup)
1 large onion, cut into thin wedges
1 8-ounce can sliced water chestnuts, drained
1 medium red sweet pepper, cut into 1-inch pieces
1 stalk celery, bias-sliced (½ cup)
2 pounds boneless pork shoulder roast, cut into 1-inch pieces
2 tablespoons packed brown sugar
2 tablespoons rice vinegar
2 tablespoons tomato paste
2 tablespoons quick-cooking tapioca, crushed
1 tablespoon reduced-sodium soy sauce
1 tablespoon sherry (optional)
2 cloves garlic, minced

½ teaspoon toasted sesame oil
3 cups hot cooked brown rice
½ cup chopped green onions (optional)

1. Drain pineapple chunks, reserving the juice; set aside pineapple chunks.
2. In a 3½- or 4-quart slow cooker, combine carrots, onion, water chestnuts, sweet pepper, and celery. Top with pork. In a medium bowl, whisk together reserved pineapple juice, the brown sugar, rice vinegar, tomato paste, tapioca, soy sauce, sherry (if desired), garlic, and sesame oil. Pour over all in cooker.
3. Cover and cook on low-heat setting for 7 to 8 hours or on high-heat setting for 3½ to 4 hours. Stir in reserved pineapple chunks. Serve over hot cooked rice. If desired, sprinkle with green onions.
PER SERVING: 342 cal., 8 g total fat (3 g sat. fat), 73 mg chol., 221 mg sodium, 41 g carb., 4 g fiber, 25 g pro. Exchanges: 1 vegetable, 0.5 fruit, 2 starch, 2.5 lean meat. Carb choices: 3.

Italian Pork Chops

The duo of Italian seasoning and balsamic vinegar lends authentic old-world flavor to these meaty chops.
SERVINGS 6 (1 pork chop, ½ cup orzo, and about ⅓ cup sauce each)
CARB. PER SERVING 29 g

1 medium onion, chopped (½ cup)
6 pork rib chops with bone, cut ½ inch thick (about 2½ pounds)
2 teaspoons dried Italian seasoning, crushed
4 cloves garlic, minced
½ teaspoon salt
¼ teaspoon black pepper
2 14.5-ounce cans no-salt-added diced tomatoes, undrained
2 tablespoons balsamic vinegar
2 medium zucchini, halved lengthwise and cut crosswise into 1-inch pieces
2 tablespoons cornstarch
2 tablespoons cold water
3 cups hot cooked orzo

1. Place onion in a 5- to 6-quart slow cooker. Place half of the pork chops on top of onion. Sprinkle with half of the Italian seasoning, garlic, salt, and pepper. Repeat layering with remaining pork chops, Italian seasoning, garlic, salt, and pepper. Top with undrained tomatoes and balsamic vinegar. Add zucchini pieces to cooker.
2. Cover and cook on low-heat setting for 8 to 9 hours or on high-heat setting for 4 to 4½ hours.
3. Using a slotted spoon and tongs, transfer meat and vegetables to a serving platter; cover to keep warm. In a medium saucepan, stir together cornstarch and the cold water; stir in cooking liquid from cooker. Cook and stir over medium heat until thickened and bubbly; cook and stir for 2 minutes more. Serve over meat and vegetables with orzo.
PER SERVING: 279 cal., 5 g total fat (2 g sat. fat), 60 mg chol., 323 mg sodium, 29 g carb., 4 g fiber, 28 g pro. Exchanges: 2 vegetable, 1 starch, 3 lean meat. Carb choices: 2.

Italian Pork Chops

No need to brown the meat here—rich red sauce bathes the chops and adds great flavor.

Greek Lamb with Spinach and Orzo

Bold Mediterranean flavors come alive in this robust dish that showcases chunks of lamb tossed with orzo. Serve it over fresh spinach and sprinkle with feta cheese.

SERVINGS 10 (about 1 cup lamb mixture, 1 cup spinach, and 1½ tablespoons cheese each)

CARB. PER SERVING 28 g

- 1 tablespoon dried oregano, crushed
- 1 tablespoon finely shredded lemon peel
- 4 cloves garlic, minced
- ½ teaspoon salt
- 3 pounds lamb stew meat
- ¼ cup lemon juice
- 12 ounces dried orzo
- 1 10-ounce bag prewashed fresh spinach, chopped
- 1 cup crumbled reduced-fat feta cheese (4 ounces)

1. In a small bowl, stir together oregano, lemon peel, garlic, and salt. Sprinkle oregano mixture evenly over lamb; rub in with your fingers. Place lamb in a 3½- or 4-quart slow cooker. Sprinkle lamb with lemon juice.

2. Cover and cook on low-heat setting for 8 to 10 hours or on high-heat setting for 4 to 5 hours.

3. Meanwhile, prepare orzo according to package directions. Stir cooked orzo into lamb mixture in cooker. Place spinach on a large serving platter. Spoon lamb mixture over the spinach. Sprinkle with feta cheese. Serve with *lemon wedges*.

PER SERVING: 347 cal., 10 g total fat (4 g sat. fat), 92 mg chol., 417 mg sodium, 28 g carb., 2 g fiber, 36 g pro. Exchanges: 1 vegetable, 1.5 starch, 4 lean meat. Carb choices: 2.

Greek Braised Lamb Chops

Olives, lemon, and favorite Greek herbs—rosemary, marjoram, and thyme—season tender chops.

SERVINGS 6 (1 chop, ¾ cup bean mixture, and about ½ cup arugula each)

CARB. PER SERVING 18 g

- ½ teaspoon salt
- ½ teaspoon dried rosemary, crushed
- ½ teaspoon dried marjoram, crushed
- ¼ teaspoon dried thyme, crushed
- ½ teaspoon finely shredded lemon peel
- ¼ teaspoon black pepper
- ⅛ teaspoon crushed red pepper
- 6 lamb loin chops, cut 1½ inches thick (about 1¾ pounds)
- 1 15-ounce can cannellini beans, rinsed and drained
- 1 14.5-ounce can diced tomatoes, undrained
- 1 large onion, cut into thin wedges
- ¼ cup kalamata olives, quartered
- 1 tablespoon lemon juice
- 2 cloves garlic, minced
- 1 tablespoon olive oil
- 6 cups arugula, coarsely chopped
- 1 teaspoon lemon juice
- Herbed Goat Cheese (page 81)

1. In a small bowl, combine ¼ teaspoon of the salt, the rosemary, marjoram, thyme, lemon peel, black pepper, and crushed red pepper. Sprinkle herb mixture on lamb chops; rub in with your fingers.

2. In a 3½- to 4-quart slow cooker, place lamb chops, cannellini beans, undrained tomatoes, onion, olives, lemon juice, garlic, and remaining ¼ teaspoon salt.

3. Cover and cook on low-heat setting for 5 to 6 hours or on high-heat setting for 2½ to 3 hours.

4. Before serving, heat olive oil in a very large skillet; add arugula. Cook briefly to wilt. Add lemon juice. To

Greek Lamb with Spinach and Orzo

serve, place a chop and some of the bean mixture on a plate; serve with arugula and top with Herbed Goat Cheese.

HERBED GOAT CHEESE: In a small bowl, combine 2 ounces goat cheese and 2 teaspoons snipped fresh mint.

PER SERVING: 272 cal., 11 g total fat (4 g sat. fat), 75 mg chol., 614 mg sodium, 18 g carb., 6 g fiber, 30 g pro. Exchanges: 1 vegetable, 1 starch, 3.5 lean meat. Carb choices: 1.

Moroccan
Lamb Tagine

Moroccan Lamb Tagine

Tagine (tay-jean) is the name of savory Moroccan meat or poultry stews as well as the ceramic vessel in which they are cooked. A slow cooker creates the same kind of moist, gentle cooking environment.

SERVINGS 6 (1 cup lamb mixture and ⅓ cup couscous each)
CARB. PER SERVING 40 g

½ teaspoon ground ginger
½ teaspoon ground cumin
½ teaspoon salt
¼ teaspoon ground turmeric
¼ teaspoon ground cinnamon
1½ to 2 pounds boneless lamb shoulder roast or lamb stew meat, cut into 1-inch pieces
1½ cups coarsely chopped, peeled sweet potato
1 medium roma tomato, chopped
2 medium carrots, cut into 1-inch pieces (1 cup)
1 medium onion, chopped (½ cup)
¼ cup pitted dates, quartered
¼ cup pitted green olives, halved
2 tablespoons quick-cooking tapioca
½ teaspoon finely shredded lemon peel
1 tablespoon lemon juice
1 tablespoon honey
2 cloves garlic, minced
1 14-ounce can reduced-sodium chicken broth
2 cups hot cooked whole wheat couscous
¼ cup toasted sliced almonds

1. In a bowl, combine ginger, cumin, salt, turmeric, and cinnamon. Add lamb to bowl; toss to coat.
2. In a 3½- or 4-quart slow cooker, place lamb, sweet potato, tomato, carrots, onion, dates, olives, tapioca, lemon peel, lemon juice, honey, and garlic. Pour broth over all.
3. Cover and cook on low-heat setting for 8 to 10 hours or on high-heat setting for 4 to 5 hours.
4. Serve over hot cooked couscous and top with almonds.

PER SERVING: 343 cal., 9 g total fat (2 g sat. fat), 69 mg chol., 562 mg sodium, 40 g carb., 6 g fiber, 28 g pro. Exchanges: 0.5 vegetable, 2.5 starch, 3 lean meat. Carb choices: 2.5.

Spiced Lamb with Curried Slaw

*This main dish comes with a side-dish bonus:
a crisp, refreshing slaw that contrasts with
the complex flavors of the lamb.*

SERVINGS 8 (½ cup meat and ½ cup slaw each)
CARB. PER SERVING 10 g

- 1 2½- to 3-pound boneless lamb shoulder roast
- 1 medium onion, cut into thin wedges
- ¼ teaspoon black pepper
- ¼ cup lower-sodium beef broth
- ¼ cup low-sugar apricot preserves
- ¼ cup reduced-sodium soy sauce
- 1 teaspoon curry powder
- 1 teaspoon finely shredded lemon peel
- ½ teaspoon ground cinnamon
- ¼ teaspoon cayenne pepper
   Curried Slaw (below)

1. Trim fat from roast. If necessary, cut roast to fit in a
3½- or 4-quart slow cooker. Place onion in cooker. Add
roast. Sprinkle with black pepper. In a small bowl,
combine broth, preserves, soy sauce, curry powder,
lemon peel, cinnamon, and cayenne pepper. Pour over
all in cooker.
2. Cover and cook on low-heat setting for 10 to 12 hours
or on high-heat setting for 5 to 6 hours.
3. Remove meat and onion from cooker, reserving
cooking liquid. Using two forks, shred meat; discard fat.
Transfer meat and onion to a serving bowl. Skim fat
from reserved liquid. Drizzle meat with enough of the
cooking liquid to moisten. Serve with Curried Slaw.
CURRIED SLAW: In a large bowl, combine ½ cup light
mayonnaise, 3 tablespoons milk, and ½ teaspoon curry
powder. Add 5 cups shredded cabbage or one 10-ounce
package shredded cabbage with carrot (coleslaw mix);
stir to coat. Cover and chill for up to 12 hours.
PER SERVING: 263 cal., 11 g total fat (3 g sat. fat), 95 mg chol.,
487 mg sodium, 10 g carb., 2 g fiber, 30 g pro. Exchanges:
1 vegetable, 0.5 starch, 3.5 lean meat. Carb choices: 0.5.

Irish Stew

*Tapioca is an excellent thickener for use in the slow cooker.
The easiest way to crush it is to use a mortar and pestle.
It you don't have them, place the tapioca between layers of
waxed paper and crush it with a rolling pin.*

SERVINGS 6 (1⅓ cups each)
CARB. PER SERVING 22 g

- 1 pound lean boneless lamb
- 1 tablespoon cooking oil
- 2 medium turnips, peeled and cut into ½-inch pieces
- 3 medium carrots, cut into ½-inch pieces
- 2 medium potatoes, peeled and cut into ½-inch pieces
- 2 medium onions, cut into thin wedges
- ¼ cup quick-cooking tapioca, crushed
- ½ teaspoon salt
- ¼ teaspoon black pepper
- ¼ teaspoon dried thyme, crushed
- 2 14-ounce cans lower-sodium beef broth

1. Trim fat from meat. Cut meat into 1-inch pieces. In a
large skillet, brown meat, half at a time, in hot oil over
medium heat. Drain off fat.
2. In a 3½- or 4-quart slow cooker, combine meat,
turnips, carrots, potatoes, onions, tapioca, salt, pepper,
and thyme. Pour broth over mixture in cooker.
3. Cover and cook on low-heat setting for 10 to 11 hours
or on high-heat setting for 5 to 5½ hours.
PER SERVING: 213 cal., 5 g total fat (1 g sat. fat), 49 mg chol.,
537 mg sodium, 22 g carb., 3 g fiber, 19 g pro. Exchanges:
1 vegetable, 1 starch, 2 lean meat. Carb choices: 1.5.

Veal Osso Buco

*Like the traditional Italian meal, this tender veal dish
features fabulous wine and garlic flavors.*

SERVINGS 6 (about 7 ounces meat with
bone, ¼ cup tomatoes, and about
2½ tablespoons Gremolata each)
CARB. PER SERVING 8 g

- 2½ to 3 pounds veal shank cross cuts (4 to 6)
- 1 tablespoon cooking oil
- 2 14.5-ounce cans no-salt-added diced tomatoes
- ½ cup dry red wine
- 2 teaspoons Italian seasoning, crushed
- 2 cloves garlic, minced
   Gremolata (page 83)

Veal Osso Buco

1. In a large skillet, brown veal, half at a time, in hot oil over medium-high heat, turning once. Drain off fat. Place veal in a 3½- or 4-quart slow cooker. In a medium bowl, combine *undrained* tomatoes, wine, Italian seasoning, and garlic. Pour over veal in cooker.

2. Cover and cook on low-heat setting for 8 to 9 hours or on high-heat setting for 4 to 4½ hours.

3. Using a slotted spoon, transfer meat and tomatoes to a serving dish. Sprinkle with Gremolata to serve.

GREMOLATA: In a small bowl, stir together ½ cup snipped fresh parsley, 2 teaspoons finely shredded lemon peel, and 2 cloves garlic, minced.

PER SERVING: 213 cal., 6 g total fat (1 g sat. fat), 99 mg chol., 171 mg sodium, 8 g carb., 3 g fiber, 27 g pro. Exchanges: 1 vegetable, 3.5 lean meat, 1 fat. Carb choices: 0.5.

Cuban-Style Black Beans and Rice

Cuban-Style Black Beans and Rice

Garlic, lime, and jalapeño chiles add sass to everyday beans and rice.

SERVINGS 6 (⅓ cup rice and ⅔ cup bean mixture each)

CARB. PER SERVING 50 g

1½ cups dry black beans, rinsed and drained
3 cups reduced-sodium chicken broth
1 large onion, chopped (1 cup)
2 bay leaves
1 to 2 fresh jalapeño chile peppers, seeded and finely chopped*
4 cloves garlic, minced
2 teaspoons ground cumin
2 teaspoons finely shredded lime peel
¼ teaspoon salt
¼ teaspoon black pepper
2 cups hot cooked brown rice
3 tablespoons snipped fresh cilantro
1 small fresh jalapeño chile pepper, seeded and chopped*
1 medium tomato, seeded and chopped
¼ cup chopped onion
Lime wedges

1. In a large saucepan, combine 4 cups water and the beans. Bring to boiling; reduce heat. Simmer, uncovered, for 10 minutes. Remove from heat. Cover and let stand for 1 hour. Drain and rinse beans.

2. Place beans in a 3½- or 4-quart slow cooker. Add broth, the 1 cup chopped onion, the bay leaves, finely chopped chile peppers, garlic, cumin, lime peel, salt, and black pepper.

3. Cover and cook on low-heat setting for 10 to 12 hours or on high-heat setting for 5 to 6 hours.

4. Drain beans, reserving cooking liquid. Discard bay leaves. Mash beans slightly. Stir in enough cooking liquid (about ½ cup) to moisten. Serve beans with hot cooked rice. Top with cilantro, chopped chiles, tomato, and the ¼ cup chopped onion. Serve with lime wedges.

***TEST KITCHEN TIP:** Because chile peppers contain volatile oils that can burn your skin and eyes, avoid direct contact with chiles as much as possible. When working with chiles, wear plastic or rubber gloves. If your bare hands do touch the chiles, wash your hands well with soap and water.

PER SERVING: 266 cal., 2 g total fat (0 g sat. fat), 0 mg chol., 393 mg sodium, 50 g carb., 10 g fiber, 14 g pro. Exchanges: 0.5 vegetable, 3 starch, 0.5 lean meat. Carb choices: 3.

Ratatouille with Lentils

Ratatouille with Lentils

Ratatouille typically features eggplant, tomatoes, sweet peppers, and summer squash or zucchini. This version adds wholesome, calcium-rich lentils.

SERVINGS 6 (1⅓ cups each)

CARB. PER SERVING 37 g

1 cup dry lentils, rinsed and drained
1 small eggplant (12 ounces), peeled and cubed
2 14.5-ounce cans no-salt-added diced tomatoes, undrained
2 large onions, coarsely chopped (2 cups)
2 medium yellow summer squash and/or zucchini, halved lengthwise and cut in ½-inch-thick slices (about 2½ cups)
1 medium red sweet pepper, chopped (¾ cup)
½ cup water
1 tablespoon Italian seasoning, crushed
2 cloves garlic, minced
½ teaspoon salt
¼ to ½ teaspoon black pepper

1. In a 3½- or 4-quart slow cooker, combine lentils, eggplant, undrained tomatoes, onions, summer squash, sweet pepper, the water, Italian seasoning, garlic, salt, and black pepper. Cover and cook on low-heat setting for 8 to 9 hours or on high-heat setting for 4 to 4½ hours.

PER SERVING: 191 cal., 1 g total fat (0 g sat. fat), 0 mg chol., 256 mg sodium, 37 g carb., 16 g fiber, 11 g pro. Exchanges: 2 vegetable, 2 starch. Carb choices: 2.5.

Because the slow cooker needs to be at least half full to cook properly, many recipes make several servings. Do you know what that means? Leftovers for lunch tomorrow.

Hot-and-Spicy Braised Peanut Chicken

Hot-and-Spicy Braised Peanut Chicken

Look for red curry paste and light coconut milk in the Asian foods section of your supermarket.

SERVINGS 8 (about 1 cup chicken mixture and ½ cup rice each)
CARB. PER SERVING 37 g

 2 medium onions, cut into thin wedges
 3 medium carrots, sliced (1½ cups)
 1 small red sweet pepper, cut into bite-size strips
 2 pounds skinless, boneless chicken thighs, cut into 1-inch pieces
 ¾ cup reduced-sodium chicken broth
 3 tablespoons creamy peanut butter
 ½ teaspoon finely shredded lime peel
 2 tablespoons lime juice
 2 tablespoons reduced-sodium soy sauce
 2 tablespoons quick-cooking tapioca
 1 tablespoon grated fresh ginger
 2 to 3 teaspoons red curry paste
 4 cloves garlic, minced
 ½ cup unsweetened light coconut milk
 1 cup frozen peas
 4 cups hot cooked brown rice
 ¼ cup chopped unsalted peanuts
    Snipped fresh cilantro (optional)

1. In a 3½- or 4-quart slow cooker, place onions, carrots, and sweet pepper. Top with chicken. In a medium bowl, whisk together broth, peanut butter, lime peel, lime juice, soy sauce, tapioca, ginger, curry paste, and garlic until smooth. Pour over all in cooker.
2. Cover and cook on low-heat setting for 5 to 6 hours or on high-heat setting for 2½ to 3 hours. Stir in coconut milk and peas. Let stand, covered, for 5 minutes.
3. Serve chicken mixture over hot cooked rice. Sprinkle individual servings with chopped peanuts and, if desired, cilantro.

PER SERVING: 372 cal., 12 g total fat (3 g sat. fat), 94 mg chol., 379 mg sodium, 37 g carb., 4 g fiber, 30 g pro. Exchanges: 1 vegetable, 2 starch, 3 lean meat, 0.5 fat. Carb choices: 2.5.

Italian Braised Chicken with Fennel and Cannellini

Use a vegetable peeler or a cheese cutter to make large shavings from a chunk of Parmesan.

SERVINGS 6 (1 to 2 pieces chicken and 1 cup bean mixture each)

CARB. PER SERVING 23 g

- 2 to 2½ pounds chicken drumsticks and/or thighs, skinned
- ¼ teaspoon salt
- ¼ teaspoon black pepper
- 1 15-ounce can cannellini beans, rinsed and drained
- 1 medium fennel bulb, cored and cut into thin wedges
- 1 medium yellow sweet pepper, cut into 1-inch pieces
- 1 medium onion, cut into thin wedges
- 3 cloves garlic, minced
- 1 teaspoon snipped fresh rosemary or ½ teaspoon dried rosemary, crushed
- 1 teaspoon snipped fresh oregano or ½ teaspoon dried oregano, crushed
- ¼ teaspoon crushed red pepper
- 1 14.5-ounce can diced tomatoes, undrained
- ½ cup dry white wine or reduced-sodium chicken broth
- ¼ cup tomato paste
- ¼ cup shaved Parmesan cheese (1 ounce)
- 1 tablespoon snipped fresh Italian (flat-leaf) parsley

1. Sprinkle chicken pieces with salt and pepper. Place chicken in a 3½- to 4-quart slow cooker. Top with cannellini beans, fennel, sweet pepper, onion, garlic, rosemary, oregano, and crushed red pepper. In a medium bowl, combine undrained tomatoes, white wine, and tomato paste. Pour over all in cooker.

2. Cover and cook on low-heat setting for 5 to 6 hours or on high-heat setting for 2½ to 3 hours.

3. Sprinkle individual servings with Parmesan cheese and parsley.

PER SERVING: 225 cal., 4 g total fat (1 g sat. fat), 68 mg chol., 584 mg sodium, 23 g carb., 7 g fiber, 25 g pro. Exchanges: 0.5 vegetable, 1.5 starch, 3 very lean meat. Carb choices: 1.5.

Soy-Ginger Soup with Chicken

Dried Japanese somen noodles look like angel hair pasta. Look for them wrapped in bundles in the ethnic section of your local supermarket.

SERVINGS 6 (1¼ cups each)
CARB. PER SERVING 12 g

- 1 pound skinless, boneless chicken thighs, cut into 1-inch pieces
- 1 cup coarsely shredded carrots
- 2 tablespoons dry sherry (optional)
- 1 tablespoon reduced-sodium soy sauce
- 1 tablespoon rice vinegar
- 1 teaspoon grated fresh ginger or ½ teaspoon ground ginger
- ¼ teaspoon black pepper
- 1 14-ounce can reduced-sodium chicken broth
- 4½ cups water
- 2 ounces dried somen noodles
- 1 6-ounce package frozen snow pea pods, thawed
- Snipped fresh cilantro (optional)

1. In a 3½- to 6-quart slow cooker, combine chicken, carrots, sherry (if desired), soy sauce, vinegar, ginger, and pepper. Stir in broth and the water.

2. Cover and cook on high-heat setting for 2 to 3 hours. Stir in noodles and pea pods. Cover and cook for 3 minutes more.

3. To serve, ladle soup into bowls. If desired, garnish with cilantro.

PER SERVING: 151 cal., 3 g total fat (1 g sat. fat), 63 mg chol., 505 mg sodium, 12 g carb., 2 g fiber, 18 g pro. Exchanges: 0.5 vegetable, 0.5 starch, 2.5 lean meat. Carb choices: 1.

Chinese Chicken Salad

Many chain restaurants serve an Asian-inspired chicken salad. Tonight drive past them all because a slow-cooked version is waiting at home. This recipe makes plenty, so it's ideal for a brunch or lunch gathering.

SERVINGS 6 to 8
CARB. PER SERVING 16 g

- 2 pounds chicken thighs, skinned
  Black pepper
- 2 stalks celery, chopped (1 cup)
- 1 medium onion, chopped (½ cup)
- 2 cloves garlic, minced
- ½ cup bottled hoisin sauce
- 2 tablespoons reduced-sodium soy sauce
- 2 tablespoons grated fresh ginger
- 1 tablespoon dry sherry
- 2 teaspoons Asian chili sauce
- 1 teaspoon toasted sesame oil
- ¼ cup rice vinegar
- 8 cups shredded romaine lettuce
- 2 medium carrots, shredded (1 cup)
- ⅓ cup unsalted dry-roasted cashews
- 2 tablespoons snipped fresh cilantro

1. Sprinkle chicken with pepper. Place chicken in a 3- to 4-quart slow cooker. Add celery, onion, and garlic. In a small bowl, combine hoisin sauce, soy sauce, ginger, sherry, chili sauce, and sesame oil. Stir into mixture in cooker.
2. Cover and cook on low-heat setting for 5 to 6 hours or on high-heat setting for 2½ to 3 hours.
3. Using a slotted spoon, transfer chicken to a cutting board, reserving ½ cup of the cooking liquid. When chicken is cool enough to handle, remove chicken from bones; discard bones. Using two forks, shred chicken.
4. For dressing: In a screw-top jar, combine the reserved ½ cup cooking liquid and the rice vinegar. Cover and shake until combined; set aside.
5. In a large salad bowl, combine chicken, romaine, carrots, cashews, and cilantro. Before serving, shake dressing and drizzle over salad. Toss to coat.
PER SERVING: 230 cal., 9 g total fat (2 g sat. fat), 71 mg chol., 584 mg sodium, 16 g carb., 3 g fiber, 21 g pro. Exchanges: 1.5 vegetable, 0.5 starch, 2.5 very lean meat, 1 fat. Carb choices: 1.

Chicken Tostadas

Another time, roll up the zippy chicken in whole wheat tortillas like burritos and serve them with all the toppings.

SERVINGS 10 (1 tostada each)
CARB. PER SERVING 24 g

- 2 fresh jalapeño chile peppers, seeded and finely chopped*
- 8 cloves garlic, minced
- 3 tablespoons chili powder
- 3 tablespoons lime juice
- ¼ teaspoon bottled hot pepper sauce
- 1 medium onion, sliced and separated into rings
- 2 pounds skinless, boneless chicken thighs
- 1 16-ounce can fat-free refried beans
- 10 purchased tostada shells
- ¾ cup shredded reduced-fat cheddar cheese (3 ounces)
- 2 cups shredded lettuce
- ¾ cup bottled salsa
- ¾ cup light sour cream
- ½ cup sliced ripe olives

1. In a 3½- to 5-quart slow cooker, combine chile peppers, garlic, chili powder, lime juice, and hot pepper sauce. Add onion and chicken.
2. Cover and cook on low-heat setting for 5 to 6 hours or on high-heat setting for 2½ to 3 hours.
3. Remove chicken and onion from cooker, reserving ½ cup of the cooking liquid. Using two forks, shred chicken. In a medium bowl, combine chicken, onion, and the ½ cup cooking liquid.
4. Spread refried beans on tostada shells. Top with hot chicken mixture and shredded cheese. Serve with lettuce, salsa, sour cream, and olives.
*TEST KITCHEN TIP: Because hot chile peppers contain volatile oils that can burn your skin and eyes, avoid direct contact with chiles as much as possible. When working with chiles, wear plastic or rubber gloves. If your bare hands do touch the chiles, wash your hands well with soap and water.
PER SERVING: 290 cal., 10 g total fat (4 g sat. fat), 86 mg chol., 615 mg sodium, 24 g carb., 5 g fiber, 25 g pro. Exchanges: 1.5 starch, 3 very lean meat, 1 fat. Carb choices: 1.5.

Coq au Vin Stew

2. Place chicken thighs in a 3½- or 4-quart slow cooker. Sprinkle chicken with dry soup mix. Add mushrooms, onions, and carrots. Pour wine over all in cooker.
3. Cover and cook on low-heat setting for 5 to 6 hours or on high-heat setting for 2½ to 3 hours. Serve with mashed potatoes and sprinkle with parsley.
PER SERVING: 269 cal., 6 g total fat (1 g sat. fat), 107 mg chol., 627 mg sodium, 20 g carb., 2 g fiber, 29 g pro. Exchanges: 0.5 vegetable, 1 starch, 3.5 lean meat. Carb choices: 1.

Paella with Chicken and Shrimp
A little turmeric goes a long way. This spice adds both pungent flavor and intense yellow-orange color.
SERVINGS 10
CARB. PER SERVING 36 g

 1 medium green sweet pepper, chopped (¾ cup)
 1 medium onion, chopped (½ cup)
 2 cloves garlic, minced
 3 medium tomatoes, chopped
 2 cups reduced-sodium chicken broth
 1 cup water
 2 teaspoons dried oregano, crushed
 ½ teaspoon salt
 ½ teaspoon ground turmeric
 ½ teaspoon black pepper
 ½ teaspoon bottled hot pepper sauce (optional)
 3 pounds chicken thighs and drumsticks, skinned
 8 ounces smoked turkey sausage, halved lengthwise and sliced
 2 cups uncooked long grain rice
 8 ounces cooked, peeled, and deveined shrimp (tails removed)
 1 cup frozen peas

1. In a 6-quart slow cooker, combine sweet pepper, onion, garlic, tomatoes, broth, water, oregano, salt, turmeric, black pepper, and hot pepper sauce, if using. Top with chicken and sausage.
2. Cover and cook on low-heat setting for 8 to 10 hours or on high-heat setting for 4 to 5 hours. Stir in uncooked rice. If using low-heat setting, turn to high-heat setting. Cover and cook for 30 to 45 minutes more or until rice is tender. Stir in cooked shrimp and peas. Let stand, covered, for 10 minutes.
PER SERVING: 312 cal., 5 g total fat (1 g sat. fat), 121 mg chol., 568 mg sodium, 36 g carb., 2 g fiber, 28 g pro. Exchanges: 1 vegetable, 2 starch, 3 very lean meat. Carb choices: 2.5.

Coq au Vin Stew
Beefy onion soup mix and red wine combine with chicken for a stew that's luscious and comforting on a cold night.
SERVINGS 6
CARB. PER SERVING 20 g

    Nonstick cooking spray
 3 pounds chicken thighs, skinned
 1 envelope (½ of a 2.2-ounce package) beefy onion soup mix
 2 cups quartered fresh mushrooms
1½ cups frozen small whole onions
 3 medium carrots, cut into 3×½-inch sticks
 ½ cup dry red wine
 2 cups hot cooked mashed potatoes
    Snipped fresh parsley

1. Lightly coat a large skillet with cooking spray. Heat skillet over medium heat. Cook chicken thighs, several at a time, in the hot skillet until browned. Drain off fat.

Chinese Red-Cooked Chicken

Red cooking is a Chinese method of braising poultry in a flavorful liquid that includes soy sauce and caramelized sugar. The meat takes on a beautiful red-brown color.

SERVINGS 6 (4½ ounces meat, ½ cup noodles, and about ¼ cup cooking liquid each)

CARB. PER SERVING 24 g

2½ to 3 pounds chicken drumsticks and/or thighs, skinned
3 whole star anise
2 3-inch-long strips orange peel*
1 2-inch piece fresh ginger, thinly sliced
3 inches stick cinnamon
2 cloves garlic, smashed
1 teaspoon whole Szechwan peppercorns or black peppercorns
2 green onions, cut into 2-inch pieces
1 cup reduced-sodium chicken broth
2 tablespoons reduced-sodium soy sauce
2 teaspoons packed brown sugar
1 teaspoon dry sherry (optional)
1 8-ounce package Chinese egg noodles
2 tablespoons fresh cilantro leaves

1. Place chicken in a 3½- or 4-quart slow cooker. For the spice bag, cut an 8-inch square from a double-thickness of 100-percent-cotton cheesecloth. In center of the square, place star anise, orange peel, ginger, cinnamon, garlic, and peppercorns. Gather corners and tie closed with 100-percent-cotton kitchen string. Add to slow cooker. Top with green onions. In a bowl, combine broth, soy sauce, brown sugar, and, if desired, sherry. Pour over all in cooker.

2. Cover and cook on low-heat setting for 6 to 7 hours or on high-heat setting for 3 to 3½ hours.

3. Meanwhile, prepare noodles according to package directions. Remove chicken from cooking liquid. Strain liquid, discarding spice bag and solids; skim off fat. Serve chicken over hot cooked noodles in shallow bowls. Drizzle chicken and noodles with cooking liquid and garnish with cilantro leaves.

*TEST KITCHEN TIP: Use a vegetable peeler to remove 3-inch-long strips of peel from an orange, avoiding the bitter white pith underneath.

PER SERVING: 244 cal., 4 g total fat (1 g sat. fat), 90 mg chol., 576 mg sodium, 24 g carb., 1 g fiber, 26 g pro. Exchanges: 1.5 starch, 3 lean meat. Carb choices: 1.5.

Chinese Red-Cooked Chicken

Mole with Chicken and Rice

In this chicken-and-rice favorite, mole—a spicy sauce made with chiles and chocolate—wows the taste buds. For an authentic Mexican garnish, sprinkle on toasted pepitas (pumpkin seeds) instead of almonds.

SERVINGS 6 (3 ounces cooked chicken and ⅓ cup rice each)
CARB. PER SERVING 30 g

- 1 14.5-ounce can diced tomatoes, undrained
- 1 medium onion, chopped (½ cup)
- ¼ cup slivered almonds, toasted
- 3 cloves garlic, quartered
- 2 tablespoons canned chopped jalapeño chile peppers, drained
- 3 tablespoons raisins
- 2 tablespoons unsweetened cocoa powder
- 1 tablespoon sesame seeds
- ¼ teaspoon salt
- ¼ teaspoon ground cinnamon
- ⅛ teaspoon ground nutmeg
- ⅛ teaspoon ground coriander
- Nylon slow cooker liner or nonstick cooking spray
- 2 tablespoons quick-cooking tapioca
- 1 2½- to 3-pound broiler-fryer chicken, cut up and skinned
- 2 tablespoons slivered almonds, toasted
- 2 cups hot cooked brown rice

1. For mole: In a blender or food processor, combine undrained tomatoes, onion, the ¼ cup almonds, the garlic, chile peppers, raisins, cocoa powder, sesame seeds, salt, cinnamon, nutmeg, and coriander. Cover and blend or process until mixture is a coarse puree.
2. Line a 3½- or 4-quart slow cooker with a slow cooker liner or coat slow cooker with cooking spray. Place tapioca in cooker. Add chicken. Pour mole over chicken.
3. Cover and cook on low-heat setting for 9 to 10 hours or on high-heat setting for 4½ to 5 hours.
4. Transfer chicken to a serving platter. Stir sauce; pour sauce over chicken. Sprinkle with the 2 tablespoons almonds. Serve with hot cooked rice.
PER SERVING: 287 cal., 8 g total fat (1 g sat. fat), 63 mg chol., 331 mg sodium, 30 g carb., 3 g fiber, 24 g pro. Exchanges: 0.5 vegetable, 1.5 starch, 2.5 lean meat. Carb choices: 2.

Puttanesca Chicken

Capers and olives give this sauce its spirited Italian angle. If you prefer, substitute your favorite pasta for the tiny almond-shaped orzo.

SERVINGS 6
CARB. PER SERVING 31 g

- 2½ to 3 pounds meaty chicken pieces (breast halves, thighs, and drumsticks), skinned
- ⅛ teaspoon black pepper
- 1 26-ounce jar pasta sauce with olives
- 2 tablespoons drained capers
- 1 teaspoon finely shredded lemon peel
- 3 cups hot cooked orzo

1. Place chicken in a 3½- or 4-quart slow cooker. Sprinkle with pepper. In a medium bowl, stir together pasta sauce, capers, and lemon peel. Pour over chicken.
2. Cover and cook on low-heat setting for 6 to 7 hours or on high-heat setting for 3 to 3½ hours. Serve chicken and sauce over hot cooked orzo.
PER SERVING: 286 cal., 4 g total fat (1 g sat. fat), 78 mg chol., 540 mg sodium, 31 g carb., 3 g fiber, 31 g pro. Exchanges: 2 starch, 3.5 very lean meat. Carb choices: 2.

Moroccan Chicken Stew

Moroccan cooking often includes fruit, such as raisins and dried apricots, in savory meat and vegetable dishes. It's an exotic taste you'll love.

SERVINGS 6 (1 piece chicken, about ½ cup sauce, and ⅓ cup couscous each)
CARB. PER SERVING 41 g

- 2 cups sliced carrots (4 medium)
- 2 large onions, halved and thinly sliced
- 6 small chicken breast halves (2½ to 3 pounds), skinned
- ½ teaspoon salt
- ⅓ cup raisins
- ⅓ cup dried apricots, coarsely chopped
- 1 14-ounce can reduced-sodium chicken broth
- ¼ cup tomato paste
- 2 tablespoons all-purpose flour
- 2 tablespoons lemon juice
- 2 cloves garlic, minced
- 1½ teaspoons ground cumin
- 1½ teaspoons ground ginger
- 1 teaspoon ground cinnamon
- ¾ teaspoon black pepper

Dried fruit and a unique blend of spices give Moroccan dishes complex, tongue-tingling flavor.

Moroccan
Chicken Stew

2 cups hot cooked whole wheat couscous
3 tablespoons pine nuts, toasted
 Fresh cilantro sprigs

1. In a 5- to 6-quart slow cooker, place carrots and onions. Sprinkle chicken with salt; add to cooker. Top chicken with raisins and apricots. In a medium bowl, whisk together broth, tomato paste, flour, lemon juice, garlic, cumin, ginger, cinnamon, and pepper. Pour over all in cooker.

2. Cover and cook on low-heat setting for 6½ to 7 hours or on high-heat setting for 3½ to 4 hours.
3. Serve stew in shallow bowls with hot cooked couscous. Sprinkle with pine nuts and garnish with cilantro.
PER SERVING: 338 cal., 5 g total fat, (1 g sat. fat), 71 mg chol., 535 mg sodium, 41 g carb., 6 g fiber, 35 g pro. Exchanges: 1 vegetable, 0.5 fruit, 1.5 starch, 4 lean meat. Carb choices: 3.

big meaty
sandwiches

Jerk Pork Wraps
with Lime Mayo

Who needs takeout from a sandwich shop when something fresh-cooked and better for you waits at home? Fill a slow cooker with seasoned pork, saucy beef, or herbed chicken early in the day. After hours of slow simmering, spoon it on a bun or wrap it in a tortilla to enjoy.

Jerk Pork Wraps with Lime Mayo

A creamy lime dressing provides a cooling counterpoint to gutsy jerk-seasoned pork.

SERVINGS 6 (1 wrap each)
CARB. PER SERVING 24 g

1   1½- to 2-pound boneless pork shoulder roast
1   tablespoon Jamaican jerk seasoning
¼   teaspoon dried thyme, crushed
1   cup water
1   tablespoon lime juice
6   8-inch flour tortillas
6   lettuce leaves (optional)
½   cup chopped red or green sweet pepper
1   medium mango, peeled, seeded, and chopped, or 1 cup chopped pineapple
Lime Mayo (below)

1. Trim fat from roast. Sprinkle jerk seasoning evenly over roast; rub in with your fingers. Place roast in a 3½- or 4-quart slow cooker. Sprinkle with thyme. Pour the 1 cup water over roast in cooker.

2. Cover and cook on low-heat setting for 8 to 10 hours or on high-heat setting for 4 to 5 hours.

3. Remove meat from cooker; discard cooking liquid. Using two forks, shred meat; discard fat. Place meat in a medium bowl. Stir lime juice into meat.

4. If desired, line tortillas with lettuce leaves. Spoon ½ cup meat mixture onto the center of each tortilla. Top with about 1 tablespoon sweet pepper, 2 to 3 tablespoons mango, and about 2 tablespoons Lime Mayo. Fold up the bottom of each tortilla; fold in sides. Roll up and serve immediately.

LIME MAYO: In a small bowl, stir together ½ cup light mayonnaise, ¼ cup finely chopped red onion, ¼ teaspoon finely shredded lime peel, 1 tablespoon lime juice, and 1 clove garlic, minced. Cover and store in refrigerator until ready to serve or for up to 1 week.

PER SERVING: 343 cal., 16 g total fat (4 g sat. fat), 80 mg chol., 501 mg sodium, 24 g carb., 2 g fiber, 25 g pro. Exchanges: 1.5 starch, 3 lean meat, 1 fat. Carb choices: 1.5.

Asian Pork Sandwiches

Here's a new take on a "dip" sandwich. In contrast to the classic herbed broth, this sweetly spiced juice pairs perfectly with the pork-and-cabbage combo.

SERVINGS 8 (1 sandwich and ¼ cup cooking liquid each)

CARB. PER SERVING 27 g

Asian Pork Sandwiches

1   2½- to 3-pound pork shoulder roast
1   cup apple juice or apple cider
2   tablespoons reduced-sodium soy sauce
2   tablespoons bottled hoisin sauce
1½ teaspoons five-spice powder
8   whole wheat hamburger buns, split and toasted
2   cups shredded Chinese cabbage (napa) or packaged shredded broccoli (broccoli slaw mix)

1. Trim fat from roast. If necessary, cut roast to fit in a 3½- or 4-quart slow cooker. Place roast in cooker. In a small bowl, combine apple juice, soy sauce, hoisin sauce, and five-spice powder. Pour mixture over roast in cooker.
2. Cover and cook on low-heat setting for 10 to 12 hours or on high heat setting for 5 to 6 hours.
3. Remove meat from cooker, reserving cooking liquid. Remove meat from bone; discard bone. Using two forks, shred meat; discard fat.
4. Place ½ cup meat on each bun bottom. Top with ¼ cup shredded Chinese cabbage or broccoli; add bun tops. Skim fat from cooking liquid. Serve liquid in individual bowls for dipping (¼ cup per serving).
PER SERVING: 335 cal., 9 g total fat (3 g sat. fat), 92 mg chol., 513 mg sodium, 27 g carb., 2 g fiber, 33 g pro. Exchanges: 2 starch, 4 lean meat. Carb choices: 2.

Honey BBQ Shredded Pork Wraps

Shave off a few grams of carbohydrate from your daily count by using low-carb tortillas.

SERVINGS 12 (1 wrap each)

CARB. PER SERVING 24 g

1   3- to 3½-pound boneless pork shoulder roast
1   cup ketchup
2   stalks celery, chopped (1 cup)
1   large onion, chopped (1 cup)
½   cup water
⅓   cup honey
¼   cup lemon juice
3   tablespoons white vinegar
2   tablespoons dry mustard
2   tablespoons Worcestershire sauce
½   teaspoon black pepper
12 8-inch whole wheat tortillas

1. Trim fat from roast. If necessary, cut roast to fit in a 4- to 5-quart slow cooker. Place roast in cooker. In a medium bowl, stir together ketchup, celery, onion, the water, honey, lemon juice, vinegar, mustard, Worcestershire sauce, and pepper. Pour mixture over roast in cooker.
2. Cover and cook on low-heat setting for 13 to 14 hours or on high-heat setting for 6½ to 7 hours. Remove meat from cooker, reserving sauce. Using two forks, shred meat; discard fat. Place meat in a large bowl.
3. Skim fat from sauce. Add enough of the reserved sauce to moisten meat (about 1 cup). Spoon about ⅔ cup pork on top of each tortilla. Roll up and cut in half to serve.
PER SERVING: 326 cal., 10 g total fat (3 g sat. fat), 73 mg chol., 589 mg sodium, 24 g carb., 10 g fiber, 31 g pro. Exchanges: 1.5 starch, 4 lean meat. Carb choices: 1.5.

There is an art to shredding meat. Once the meat is cool enough to handle, use two forks to pull it with the grain in opposite directions, making shreds of varying sizes.

Honey BBQ Shredded Pork Wraps

Asian Lettuce Wraps

Set out bowls of the succulent Asian-seasoned beef mixture and a platter of lettuce leaves so diners can build their own wraps.

SERVINGS 12 (2 wraps each)
CARB. PER SERVING 5 g

1	3-pound boneless beef chuck pot roast
1½	cups diced jicama or chopped celery
4	green onions, chopped (½ cup)
¼	cup rice vinegar
¼	cup reduced-sodium soy sauce
2	tablespoons bottled hoisin sauce
1	tablespoon finely chopped fresh ginger
½	teaspoon salt
½	teaspoon chili oil
¼	teaspoon black pepper
2	tablespoons cornstarch
2	tablespoons cold water
24	Bibb or Boston lettuce leaves

1. Trim fat from roast. If necessary, cut roast to fit in a 3½- or 4-quart slow cooker. Place roast in cooker. In a medium bowl, combine jicama, green onions, vinegar, soy sauce, hoisin sauce, ginger, salt, chili oil, and pepper. Pour mixture over roast in cooker.
2. Cover and cook on low-heat setting for 8 to 10 hours or on high-heat setting for 4 to 5 hours.
3. If using low-heat setting, turn to high-heat setting. In a small bowl, combine cornstarch and the water. Stir cornstarch mixture into liquid around the meat. Cover and cook about 15 minutes more or until liquid is thickened.
4. Remove meat from cooker. Using two forks, shred meat; discard fat. Return meat to cooker and stir. Spoon about ¼ cup of the meat mixture onto each lettuce leaf. Fold bottom edge of each lettuce leaf up and over filling. Fold in sides; roll up from bottom.
PER SERVING: 168 cal., 4 g total fat (1 g sat. fat), 67 mg chol., 401 mg sodium, 5 g carb., 0 g fiber, 25 g pro. Exchanges: 1 vegetable, 3 lean meat. Carb choices: 0.

Mexican-Style Pot Roast Sandwiches

If you like to load your sandwiches, pile on some shredded lettuce and add a spoonful of salsa or light sour cream.

SERVINGS 10 (1 sandwich and about 2 tablespoons onions each)
CARB. PER SERVING 34 g

1	3- to 3½-pound boneless pork shoulder roast
4	cloves garlic, thinly sliced
1½	cups vinegar
1	cup fresh cilantro leaves
1	medium onion, cut into wedges
¼	cup water
1	teaspoon dried oregano, crushed
1	teaspoon ground cumin
¼	teaspoon salt
¼	teaspoon black pepper
2	medium red onions, thinly sliced
1	tablespoon cooking oil
¼	cup lime juice
10	multigrain ciabatta rolls, split and toasted

1. Trim fat from roast. With a sharp knife, make slits evenly on all sides of the roast. Insert garlic slices into slits. Place roast in a 3½- or 4-quart slow cooker.
2. In a blender, combine vinegar, cilantro, onion wedges, the water, oregano, cumin, salt, and pepper. Cover and blend until smooth. Pour mixture over roast in cooker.
3. Cover and cook on low-heat setting for 10 to 12 hours or on high-heat setting for 5 to 6 hours.
4. Before serving, in a large skillet, cook red onions in hot oil about 15 minutes or until tender. Carefully add lime juice to skillet. Cook and stir for 3 to 5 minutes or until lime juice evaporates.
5. Meanwhile, using a slotted spoon, remove meat from cooker. Using two forks, shred meat; discard fat. Transfer shredded meat to a large bowl. Add 1 cup of the cooking liquid remaining in cooker, tossing to coat.
6. Spoon about ⅔ cup of the meat mixture onto each roll bottom. If desired, drizzle with additional cooking liquid. Top with cooked red onions and roll tops.
PER SERVING: 378 cal., 10 g total fat (3 g sat. fat), 88 mg chol., 496 mg sodium, 34 g carb., 3 g fiber, 32 g pro. Exchanges: 0.5 vegetable, 2 starch, 3.5 lean meat. Carb choices: 2.

Classic French Dips

Classic French Dips

It takes a sturdy loaf of bread to encase a meat filling meant for dipping. If you wish, give the cut sides of these hearty slices a quick toast under the broiler.

SERVINGS 6 (1 sandwich and about ½ cup cooking liquid each)

CARB. PER SERVING 39 g

1 large sweet onion, cut into ½-inch-thick slices and separated into rings
1 2- to 2½-pound fresh beef brisket or boneless beef bottom round roast
2 cloves garlic, minced
1 teaspoon dried thyme, marjoram, or oregano, crushed
½ teaspoon black pepper
1 14-ounce can lower-sodium beef broth
2 tablespoons Worcestershire sauce
1 16-ounce loaf whole grain baguette-style bread, cut crosswise into 6 pieces and split in half horizontally

1. Place onion rings in a 3½- to 5-quart slow cooker. Trim fat from brisket. If necessary, cut brisket to fit in cooker. Place brisket on top of onion. Sprinkle with garlic, thyme, and pepper. Pour beef broth and Worcestershire sauce over all in cooker.

2. Cover and cook on low-heat setting for 9 to 10 hours for brisket or 8 to 9 hours for bottom round or on high-heat setting for 4½ to 5 hours for brisket or 4 to 4½ hours for bottom round.

3. Remove meat from cooker; thinly slice meat across the grain, removing visible fat as you slice. Using a slotted spoon, remove onion rings from cooker. Place 3 to 4 ounces sliced brisket on top of each bread bottom. Top each with onion rings. Add bread tops. Skim fat from cooking liquid in cooker; pass liquid for dipping sandwiches (about ½ cup per serving).

PER SERVING: 339 cal., 7 g total fat (2 g sat. fat), 45 mg chol., 453 mg sodium, 39 g carb., 9 g fiber, 33 g pro. Exchanges: 2.5 starch, 3.5 lean meat. Carb choices: 2.5.

Steak Sandwiches with Ratatouille

Steak Sandwiches with Ratatouille

Although ratatouille usually contains eggplant, we've created an appealing artichoke version to serve in these bistro-style steak sandwiches. For extra color, use half of a medium yellow squash and half of a medium zucchini.

SERVINGS 8 (1 wedge each)
CARB. PER SERVING 29 g

- 1½ pounds beef flank steak
- 1 teaspoon dried Italian seasoning, crushed
- ⅛ teaspoon black pepper
- 1½ cups sliced fresh mushrooms
- 1 medium onion, finely chopped (½ cup)
- 2 cloves garlic, minced
- 1 14.5-ounce can diced tomatoes, undrained
- 2 tablespoons red wine vinegar
- 1 medium yellow summer squash or zucchini, halved lengthwise and sliced (1¼ cups)
- 1 cup red, yellow, and/or green sweet pepper strips
- 1 9-inch Italian flatbread (focaccia), split in half horizontally
- 1 6-ounce jar quartered marinated artichoke hearts, drained
- ⅓ cup finely shredded Asiago or Parmesan cheese

1. Trim fat from steak. If necessary, cut steak to fit in a 3½- or 4-quart slow cooker. Sprinkle both sides of steak with Italian seasoning and black pepper. Set aside.

2. In the cooker, combine mushrooms, onion, and garlic. Add steak. Pour undrained tomatoes and vinegar over all in cooker.

3. Cover and cook on low-heat setting for 7 to 9 hours or on high-heat setting for 3½ to 4½ hours. If using low-heat setting, turn to high-heat setting. Add squash and sweet pepper. Cover and cook for 30 minutes more.

4. Remove meat from cooker. Using two forks, shred meat. Arrange meat on bottom of focaccia. Stir artichoke hearts into vegetable mixture in cooker. Using a slotted spoon, spoon vegetables onto meat. Drizzle with enough of the cooking liquid just to moisten; sprinkle with cheese. Add top of focaccia. Cut into eight wedges to serve.

PER SERVING: 334 cal., 13 g total fat (4 g sat. fat), 44 mg chol., 475 mg sodium, 29 g carb., 3 g fiber, 25 g pro. Exchanges: 1 vegetable, 1.5 starch, 2.5 lean meat, 1 fat. Carb choices: 2.

Barbecued Beef Brisket Sandwiches

Ramp up the flavor on this saucy favorite by using the optional liquid smoke in the homemade sauce mixture.

SERVINGS 8 (1 sandwich each)
CARB. PER SERVING 28 g

- 1 2- to 2½-pound fresh beef brisket
- 1 large onion, cut into thin wedges
- 1 teaspoon chili powder
- ½ teaspoon garlic powder
- ¼ teaspoon celery seeds
- ⅛ teaspoon ground pepper
- ⅓ cup ketchup
- ⅓ cup bottled chili sauce
- 2 tablespoons packed brown sugar
- 1 tablespoon vinegar
- 1 tablespoon Worcestershire sauce
- ½ teaspoon liquid smoke (optional)
- ¼ teaspoon dry mustard
- 2 tablespoons cold water
- 1 tablespoon all-purpose flour
- 8 whole wheat hamburger buns, split and toasted

1. Trim fat from brisket. If necessary, cut brisket to fit in a 3½- or 4-quart slow cooker. Place onion in cooker. In a small bowl, combine chili powder, garlic powder, celery seeds, and pepper. Sprinkle chili powder mixture evenly over brisket; rub in with your fingers. Place brisket in cooker on top of onion.

2. In a bowl, combine ketchup, chili sauce, brown sugar, vinegar, Worcestershire sauce, liquid smoke (if using), and dry mustard. Pour over all in cooker.

3. Cover and cook on low-heat setting for 9 to 10 hours or on high-heat setting for 4½ to 5 hours.

4. Remove meat from cooker. Using a slotted spoon, remove onion from cooker and place in a small bowl, reserving cooking liquid. Skim fat from cooking liquid; measure ¾ cup of the liquid. For sauce: In a small saucepan, stir the cold water into flour; add the ¾ cup cooking liquid. Cook and stir over medium heat until thickened and bubbly; cook and stir for 1 minute more.

5. Thinly slice meat across the grain. Place about 3 ounces cooked meat on each bun bottom. Top with onion, drizzle each with about 1½ tablespoons sauce, and cover with bun tops to serve.

PER SERVING: 301 cal., 8 g total fat (2 g sat. fat), 68 mg chol., 430 mg sodium, 28 g carb., 3 g fiber, 28 g pro. Exchanges: 2 starch, 3 lean meat. Carb choices: 2.

To toast buns, broil them, cut sides up, about 3 to 4 inches from the heat for 1 to 2 minutes.

Italian Beef Sandwiches

1. Trim fat from steak. If necessary, cut steak to fit in a 1½-quart slow cooker. Place steak in cooker. Sprinkle with oregano, crushed red pepper, and garlic. Pour tomato juice over all in cooker.

2. Cover and cook on low-heat setting for 7 to 8 hours or on high-heat setting for 3½ to 4 hours. If no heat setting is available, cook for 6 to 7 hours.

3. Remove meat from cooker, reserving cooking juices. Using two forks, shred meat. If desired, stir roasted pepper strips into shredded meat. Place shredded meat on bottom French bread pieces. Drizzle enough of the cooking liquid over meat to moisten. Sprinkle shredded meat with cheese. Cover with top French bread pieces.

PER SERVING: 302 cal., 11 g total fat (5 g sat. fat), 44 mg chol., 442 mg sodium, 23 g carb., 2 g fiber, 26 g pro. Exchanges: 1.5 starch, 3 lean meat, 1 fat. Carb choices: 1.5.

Souper Sloppy Joes

Canned tomato soup, mustard, Worcestershire sauce, and chili powder make this a family-pleasing sandwich.

SERVINGS 12 (1 sandwich each)
CARB. PER SERVING 29 g

- 2 pounds lean ground beef
- 2 large onions, chopped (2 cups)
- 1 10.75-ounce can reduced-sodium, reduced-fat condensed tomato soup
- 3 tablespoons yellow mustard
- 3 tablespoons Worcestershire sauce
- 1 tablespoon chili powder
- ¼ teaspoon salt
- ¼ teaspoon black pepper
- 12 whole wheat hamburger buns, split and toasted

1. In a large skillet, cook meat and onion, half at a time, until meat is browned. Drain off fat.

2. In a 3½- or 4-quart slow cooker, combine soup, mustard, Worcestershire sauce, chili powder, salt, and pepper. Stir in meat mixture.

3. Cover and cook on low-heat setting for 6 to 7 hours or on high-heat setting for 3 to 3½ hours. Stir; spoon about ⅓ cup meat mixture onto each bun bottom. Cover with bun tops.

PER SERVING: 280 cal., 9 g total fat (3 g sat. fat), 49 mg chol., 492 mg sodium, 29 g carb., 3 g fiber, 20 g pro. Exchanges: 2 starch, 2 lean meat. Carb choices: 2.

Italian Beef Sandwiches

For authentic Italian flavor, top these herbed-beef sandwiches with bottled roasted red sweet pepper strips.

SERVINGS 2 (1 sandwich each)
CARB. PER SERVING 23 g

- 6 ounces beef flank steak
- ½ teaspoon dried oregano, crushed
- Dash crushed red pepper
- 1 clove garlic, minced
- ½ cup low-sodium tomato juice
- ¼ cup bottled roasted red sweet pepper strips (optional)
- 2 4-inch-long pieces French bread, split and toasted
- ¼ cup shredded provolone cheese (1 ounce)

Greek Sandwich Wraps

A surprising mustard-garlic mayo spread gives these wraps a flavor burst with every bite.

SERVINGS 8 (1 wrap each)
CARB. PER SERVING 19 g

1	2- to 2½-pound boneless lamb shoulder roast
4	teaspoons Greek seasoning
1	medium onion, thinly sliced
¼	cup lemon juice
½	cup light mayonnaise
1	tablespoon Dijon-style mustard
2	cloves garlic, minced
8	7- to 8-inch flour tortillas
½	cup crumbled reduced-fat feta cheese
2	cups shredded spinach
1½	cups chopped cucumber (about 1 medium)
½	cup chopped tomato (1 medium)

1. Trim fat from roast. If necessary, cut roast to fit in a 3½- or 4-quart slow cooker. Sprinkle Greek seasoning onto all sides of roast; rub in with your fingers. Place onion and roast in slow cooker. Sprinkle with lemon juice.

2. Cover and cook on low-heat setting for 8 to 10 hours or on high-heat setting for 4 to 5 hours.

3. Meanwhile, in a small bowl, combine mayonnaise, mustard, and garlic. Refrigerate until ready to use.

4. Remove meat and onion from cooker. Discard fat. Using two forks, shred meat; discard fat. If necessary, skim fat from cooking liquid in cooker. Return meat and onions to slow cooker to moisten.

5. Spread one side of each tortilla with about 1 tablespoon of the mayonnaise mixture. Using a slotted spoon, spoon a scant ½ cup meat mixture onto each tortilla. Top each serving with feta cheese, spinach, cucumber, and tomato. Roll up and serve immediately.

PER SERVING: 326 cal., 15 g total fat (4 g sat. fat), 82 mg chol., 510 mg sodium, 19 g carb., 1 g fiber, 27 g pro. Exchanges: 0.5 vegetable, 1 starch, 3 lean meat, 1 fat. Carb choices: 1.

Pesto Chicken Sandwich

Pesto Chicken Sandwich

*Dine out at home on chicken sandwich wedges
just like those served in fancy bistros. Focaccia is
available at most bakeries and supermarkets.*

SERVINGS 8 (1 wedge edge)

CARB. PER SERVING 29 g

 1 teaspoon dried Italian seasoning, crushed
¼ teaspoon black pepper
 1 pound skinless, boneless chicken breast halves
 1 large onion, thinly sliced
 8 ounces fresh mushrooms, sliced

 2 cloves garlic, minced
 1 14.5-ounce can no-salt-added diced tomatoes,
   undrained
 2 tablespoons red wine vinegar
 1 medium yellow summer squash or zucchini, halved
   lengthwise and cut into ¼-inch-thick slices
 1 cup green, red, and/or yellow sweet pepper strips
⅓ cup light mayonnaise or salad dressing
 2 tablespoons purchased basil pesto
 1 8- to 9-inch Italian flatbread (focaccia), halved
   horizontally
½ cup shredded provolone cheese (2 ounces)

1. In a small bowl, combine Italian seasoning and black pepper. Sprinkle spice mixture onto all sides of chicken; rub in with your fingers.

2. In a 3½- or 4-quart slow cooker, combine chicken, onion, mushrooms, and garlic. Pour undrained tomatoes and vinegar over all in cooker.

3. Cover and cook on low-heat setting for 4 to 5 hours or on high-heat setting for 2 to 2½ hours.

4. If using low-heat setting, turn to high-heat setting. Add squash and sweet pepper. Cover and cook for 30 minutes more.

5. Meanwhile, in a small bowl, combine mayonnaise and pesto. Spread evenly over cut sides of foccacia. Remove chicken from cooker. Thinly slice chicken. Arrange chicken slices on bottom half of foccacia. Using a slotted spoon, spoon vegetable mixture over chicken. Sprinkle with cheese. Add top half of foccacia. Cut into eight wedges to serve.

PER SERVING: 279 cal., 9 g total fat (2 g sat. fat), 47 mg chol., 409 mg sodium, 29 g carb., 2 g fiber, 22 g pro. Exchanges: 1 vegetable, 1.5 starch, 2 very lean meat, 1 fat. Carb choices: 2.

Plum-Sauced Chicken in Tortillas

Deep-colored, rich hoisin sauce imparts a sweet-and-spicy flavor to the chicken. Look for hoisin sauce in the Asian foods section of the supermarket.

SERVINGS 6 (1 roll-up each)
CARB. PER SERVING 47 g

---

1 30-ounce can whole unpitted purple plums, drained
1 cup hot-style vegetable juice
¼ cup bottled hoisin sauce
4½ teaspoons quick-cooking tapioca
2 teaspoons grated fresh ginger
¼ teaspoon salt
½ teaspoon five-spice powder
⅛ to ¼ teaspoon cayenne pepper
1¼ pounds skinless, boneless chicken thighs, cut into bite-size strips
6 7- to 8-inch flour tortillas, warmed
2 cups packaged shredded broccoli (broccoli slaw mix) or packaged shredded cabbage with carrot (coleslaw mix)

1. Remove pits from drained plums. Place plums in a blender or food processor; cover and blend or process until smooth. Transfer plums to a 3½- or 4-quart slow cooker. Stir in vegetable juice, hoisin sauce, tapioca,

ginger, salt, five-spice powder, and cayenne pepper. Stir chicken into plum mixture in cooker.

2. Cover and cook on low-heat setting for 4 to 5 hours or on high-heat setting for 2 to 2½ hours. Remove chicken from cooker, reserving cooking liquid.

3. Spoon about ⅓ cup of the chicken mixture onto each warm tortilla just below the center. Drizzle with some of the reserved liquid. Top each with ⅓ cup of the shredded broccoli. Roll up tortillas.

PER SERVING: 331 cal., 4 g total fat (1 g sat. fat), 55 mg chol., 575 mg sodium, 47 g carb., 3 g fiber, 26 g pro. Exchanges: 0.5 vegetable, 0.5 fruit, 2 starch, 3 lean meat. Carb choices: 3.

Sloppy Pizza Joes

Everyone will love this vegetable-studded turkey takeoff on the traditional loose-meat sandwiches.

SERVINGS 16 (1 sandwich each)
CARB. PER SERVING 27 g

Nonstick cooking spray
3 pounds uncooked ground turkey breast
2 14-ounce jars pizza sauce
2 cups frozen stir-fry vegetables (green, red, and yellow peppers and onions), thawed and drained
½ of a 6-ounce can tomato paste (⅓ cup)
16 whole wheat hamburger buns, split and toasted
1 cup shredded part-skim mozzarella cheese (4 ounces)

1. Coat a very large skillet with cooking spray. Heat skillet over medium-high heat. Cook turkey, half at a time, in hot skillet until turkey is no longer pink, stirring to break apart. In a 4- to 5-quart slow cooker, stir together turkey, pizza sauce, vegetables, and tomato paste.

2. Cover and cook on low-heat setting for 6 to 8 hours or on high-heat setting for 3 to 4 hours.

3. Spoon about ½ cup turkey of the mixture onto each bun bottom. Top each with 1 tablespoon shredded cheese and bun tops.

PER SERVING: 258 cal., 3 g total fat (1 g sat. fat), 59 mg chol., 433 mg sodium, 27 g carb., 3 g fiber, 28 g pro. Exchanges: 1.5 starch, 3 lean meat. Carb choices: 2.

satisfying soups and stews

Smoked Sausage-Lentil Stew

Steamy, yummy soups are longtime stars on the slow-cooker scene. Here, you'll find fresh looks at old favorites as well as some new ideas for all-day simmers. To sweeten the pot for you, we've made sure each bowl is chock-full of nutritious ingredients.

Smoked Sausage-Lentil Stew

Extra turkey sausage? Another night, cook it with sauerkraut for a German-style meal. Or stir slices into pasta sauce for a new beat on the Italian scene.

SERVINGS 6
CARB. PER SERVING 30 g

1¼	cups lentils, rinsed and drained
2	14-ounce cans reduced-sodium chicken broth
1	cup water
6	ounces smoked turkey sausage, cut into ½-inch pieces
1½	cups trimmed, coarsely chopped fennel (1 medium bulb, tops reserved)
1	medium onion, chopped (½ cup)
1	medium carrot, chopped (½ cup)
4	cloves garlic, minced
1	teaspoon dried thyme, crushed
¼	teaspoon black pepper
3	tablespoons red wine vinegar

1. In a 3½- or 4-quart slow cooker, combine lentils, broth, the water, sausage, fennel, onion, carrot, garlic, thyme, and pepper.

2. Cover and cook on low-heat setting for 8 to 10 hours or on high-heat setting for 4 to 5 hours.

3. Stir in vinegar before serving. If desired, garnish individual servings with reserved fennel tops.

PER SERVING: 212 cal., 3 g total fat (1 g sat. fat), 19 mg chol., 586 mg sodium, 30 g carb., 13 g fiber, 17 g pro. Exchanges: 0.5 vegetable, 1.5 starch, 1.5 lean meat. Carb choices: 2.

Asian Turkey and Rice Soup

*Slices of mushrooms, slivers of bok choy, and chunks
of turkey mingle in a zesty soy and ginger broth,
giving stir-fry flavors to this savory soup.*

SERVINGS 6 (1 cup each)

CARB. PER SERVING 18 g

2 14-ounce cans reduced-sodium chicken broth
1 pound turkey breast tenderloin or skinless, boneless
  chicken breast halves, cut into 1-inch pieces
2 cups sliced fresh mushrooms
1½ cups water
2 medium carrots, peeled and cut into thin bite-size strips
1 medium onion, chopped (½ cup)
2 tablespoons reduced-sodium soy sauce
2 teaspoons grated fresh ginger
4 cloves garlic, minced
1½ cups sliced bok choy
1 cup instant brown rice
½ cup chow mein noodles

1. In a 3½- or 4-quart slow cooker, stir together chicken
broth, turkey, mushrooms, the water, carrots, onion, soy
sauce, ginger, and garlic.

2. Cover and cook on low-heat setting for 7 to 8 hours or
on high-heat setting for 3½ to 4 hours.

3. If using low-heat setting, turn to high-heat setting.
Stir in bok choy and uncooked rice. Cover and cook for
10 to 15 minutes more or until rice is tender. Top each
serving with chow mein noodles.

PER SERVING: 191 cal., 3 g total fat (0 g sat. fat), 47 mg chol.,
609 mg sodium, 18 g carb., 2 g fiber, 24 g pro. Exchanges:
1 vegetable, 1 starch, 2.5 lean meat. Carb choices: 1.

> Unless the recipe says to thaw them, frozen vegetables should be added to the slow cooker directly from the freezer.

Chicken Tortilla Soup

Chicken and Vegetable Bean Soup

If you wish, save the leafy greens from the fennel, then chop some up for a colorful garnish on each bowl.

SERVINGS 6 (1⅔ cups each)
CARB. PER SERVING 30 g

- 1 cup dry Great Northern beans
- 1 large onion, chopped (1 cup)
- 1 medium fennel bulb, trimmed and cut into ½-inch pieces (1½ cups)
- 2 medium carrots, chopped (1 cup)
- 2 cloves garlic, minced
- 2 tablespoons snipped fresh parsley
- 1 teaspoon dried rosemary, crushed
- ¼ teaspoon black pepper
- 4 cups reduced-sodium chicken broth
- ½ cup water
- 2½ cups shredded or chopped cooked chicken breast
- 1 14.5-ounce can diced tomatoes, undrained

1. Rinse beans; drain. In a large saucepan, combine beans and 6 cups water. Bring to boiling; reduce heat. Simmer, uncovered, for 10 minutes. Remove from heat. Cover and let stand for 1 hour. Drain and rinse beans.
2. Meanwhile, in a 4- to 5-quart slow cooker, combine onion, fennel, carrots, garlic, parsley, rosemary, and pepper. Add beans to cooker. Pour broth and the ½ cup water over all in cooker.
3. Cover and cook on low-heat setting for 8 to 10 hours or on high-heat setting for 4 to 5 hours.
4. If using low-heat setting, turn to high-heat setting. Stir in chicken and undrained tomatoes. Cover and cook about 30 minutes more or until heated through.
PER SERVING: 252 cal., 3 g total fat (1 g sat. fat), 50 mg chol., 591 mg sodium, 30 g carb., 9 g fiber, 28 g pro. Exchanges: 1 vegetable, 1.5 starch, 3 lean meat. Carb choices: 2.

Chicken Tortilla Soup

Shout olé for this easy meal! It takes five ingredients and just a few minutes to assemble.

SERVINGS 4 (about 1½ cups each)
CARB. PER SERVING 17 g

- 1 14.5-ounce can Mexican-style stewed tomatoes, undrained
- 2 cups shredded cooked chicken (about 10 ounces)
- 2 cups frozen stir-fry vegetables (green, red, and yellow peppers and onions)
- 1 cup reduced-sodium chicken broth
- 1 cup baked tortilla chips
- Sliced fresh jalapeño chile peppers* (optional)

1. In a 3½- or 4-quart slow cooker, combine 2½ cups *water*, undrained tomatoes, chicken, frozen vegetables, and broth.
2. Cover and cook on low-heat setting for 6 to 7 hours or on high-heat setting for 3 to 3½ hours.
3. Top individual servings with tortilla chips. If desired, sprinkle with chile peppers.
*TEST KITCHEN TIP: Because hot chile peppers contain volatile oils that can burn your skin and eyes, avoid direct contact with chiles as much as possible. When working with chiles, wear plastic or rubber gloves. If your bare hands do touch the chiles, wash your hands well with soap and water.
PER SERVING: 212 cal., 5 g total fat (1 g sat. fat), 62 mg chol., 612 mg sodium, 17 g carb., 1 g fiber, 23 g pro. Exchanges: 1.5 vegetable, 0.5 starch, 2.5 lean meat, 0.5 fat. Carb choices: 1.

Wild Rice
Chicken Soup

Chicken Chili

Sometimes called white chili, this spunky version adds another dimension to the traditional bowl o' red.
SERVINGS 3 (about 1 cup each)
CARB. PER SERVING 23 g

Nonstick cooking spray
8 ounces skinless, boneless chicken breast halves, cut into 1-inch pieces
1 15-ounce can white kidney beans (cannellini beans) or Great Northern beans, rinsed and drained
¾ cup reduced-sodium chicken broth
½ cup water
¼ cup chopped onion
⅓ cup chopped green sweet pepper
½ of a small fresh jalapeño chile pepper, seeded and finely chopped*
¼ teaspoon ground cumin
¼ teaspoon dried oregano, crushed
⅛ teaspoon ground white pepper
1 clove garlic, minced
2 tablespoons chopped tomato
2 tablespoons sliced green onion
2 tablespoons shredded reduced-fat Monterey Jack cheese (½ ounce)

1. Lightly coat an unheated medium skillet with cooking spray; heat skillet over medium-high heat. Brown chicken in hot skillet; drain chicken, if necessary.
2. In a 1½-quart slow cooker, combine chicken, drained beans, broth, the water, onion, sweet pepper, chile pepper, cumin, oregano, white pepper, and garlic.
3. Cover and cook on low-heat setting for 5 to 6 hours or on high-heat setting for 2½ to 3 hours. If no heat setting is available, cook for 4 to 5 hours.
4. Sprinkle individual servings with tomato, green onion, and cheese.
*TEST KITCHEN TIP: Because hot chile peppers contain volatile oils that can burn your skin and eyes, avoid direct contact with chiles as much as possible. When working with chiles, wear plastic or rubber gloves. If your bare hands do touch the chiles, wash your hands well with soap and water.
PER SERVING: 194 cal., 2 g total fat (1 g sat. fat), 47 mg chol., 446 mg sodium, 23 g carb., 7 g fiber, 28 g pro. Exchanges: 1.5 starch, 2.5 lean meat. Carb choices: 1.5.

Wild Rice Chicken Soup

Round out the earthy flavor of the wild rice with a splash of Madeira or dry sherry—about 1 tablespoon will do.
SERVINGS 8 (1⅓ cups each)
CARB. PER SERVING 16 g

1 pound skinless, boneless chicken breast halves, cut into 1-inch pieces
2 14-ounce cans reduced-sodium chicken broth
⅓ cup uncooked wild rice, rinsed and drained
⅓ cup uncooked long grain brown rice
4 cloves garlic, minced
1 tablespoon snipped fresh thyme or 1 teaspoon dried thyme, crushed
4 cups chopped fresh tomatoes or two 14.5-ounce cans no-salt-added diced tomatoes, undrained
1 cup chopped zucchini

1. Coat an unheated large skillet with *nonstick cooking spray*; heat over medium-high heat. Brown chicken in hot skillet; drain chicken, if necessary.
2. In a 3½- or 4-quart slow cooker, combine chicken, 2 cups *water*, broth, uncooked rices, garlic, dried thyme (if using), and ¼ teaspoon *black pepper*.
3. Cover; cook on low-heat setting for 6 to 7 hours or on high-heat setting for 3 to 3½ hours. If using low-heat setting, turn to high-heat setting. Add fresh thyme (if using), tomatoes, and zucchini. Cover; cook 30 minutes.
PER SERVING: 142 cal., 1 g total fat (0 g sat. fat), 33 mg chol., 354 mg sodium, 16 g carb., 2 g fiber, 17 g pro. Exchanges: 1 vegetable, 0.5 starch, 2 lean meat. Carb choices: 1.

In-a-Hurry Chicken Curry

Frozen stew vegetables eliminate peeling and cutting, keeping prep time to a quick 15 minutes.

SERVINGS 6

CARB. PER SERVING 13 g

- 1 **16-ounce package frozen stew vegetables**
- 4 **large chicken thighs (1½ to 1¾ pounds), skinned**
- ¼ **teaspoon black pepper**
- 1 **10.75-ounce can reduced-fat and reduced-sodium condensed cream of chicken soup**
- 2 **teaspoons curry powder**
- 1 **tablespoon snipped fresh cilantro**

1. Place frozen stew vegetables in a 3½- or 4-quart slow cooker. Top with chicken. Sprinkle with pepper. In a small bowl, stir together soup and curry powder. Pour soup mixture over all in cooker.

2. Cover and cook on low-heat setting for 6 to 7 hours or on high-heat setting for 3 to 3½ hours. Remove chicken from bones and, if desired, break into large pieces. Sprinkle individual servings with cilantro.

PER SERVING: 199 cal., 6 g total fat (2 g sat. fat), 98 mg chol., 320 mg sodium, 13 g carb., 1 g fiber, 24 g pro. Exchanges: 0.5 vegetable, 0.5 starch, 3 lean meat. Carb choices: 1.

In-a-Hurry Chicken Curry

Beef and Barley Soup

*Here's a home-style winter classic.
Store extra barley in a tightly covered container
in a cool, dry place for up to a year.*
SERVINGS 6 (1½ cups each)
CARB. PER SERVING 21 g

1½ pounds boneless beef sirloin steak
 2 14-ounce cans lower-sodium beef broth
 1 14.5-ounce can stewed tomatoes, undrained
 3 medium carrots, cut into ½-inch-thick slices
 2 small onions, cut into wedges
½ cup regular barley (not quick-cooking)
 1 bay leaf
 1 teaspoon dried thyme, crushed
 2 cloves garlic, minced

1. Trim fat from steak. Cut steak into ¾-inch pieces. In a 3½- or 4-quart slow cooker, combine meat, broth, undrained tomatoes, carrots, onions, barley, ½ cup *water*, bay leaf, thyme, and garlic.
2. Cover and cook on low-heat setting for 9 to 11 hours or on high-heat setting for 4½ to 5½ hours. Discard bay leaf.
PER SERVING: 249 cal., 5 g total fat (1 g sat. fat), 53 mg chol., 461 mg sodium, 21 g carb., 4 g fiber, 28 g pro. Exchanges: 1 vegetable, 1 starch, 3 lean meat. Carb choices: 1.5.

Southwest Steak and Potato Soup

*You can create your own "house" version of this flavorful
soup by using your favorite salsa.*
SERVINGS 6 (1⅓ cups each)
CARB. PER SERVING 17 g

1½ pounds boneless beef sirloin steak, cut 1 inch thick
 2 medium potatoes, cut into 1-inch pieces
 2 cups frozen cut green beans
 1 small onion, sliced and separated into rings
1½ cups thick and chunky salsa
 1 14-ounce can lower-sodium beef broth
 1 teaspoon dried basil, crushed
 2 cloves garlic, minced
⅓ cup reduced-fat shredded Monterey Jack or reduced-fat Mexican-blend cheese (optional)

1. Trim fat from steak. Cut steak into 1-inch pieces; set aside. In a 3½- or 4-quart slow cooker, combine potatoes, green beans, and onion. Add meat. In a medium bowl, stir together salsa, broth, basil, and garlic. Pour salsa mixture over all in cooker.
2. Cover and cook on low-heat setting for 8 to 10 hours or on high-heat setting for 4 to 5 hours.
3. If desired, sprinkle individual servings with cheese.
PER SERVING: 212 cal., 4 g total fat (1 g sat. fat), 68 mg chol., 576 mg sodium, 17 g carb., 3 g fiber, 28 g pro. Exchanges: 1 vegetable, 0.5 starch, 3 lean meat. Carb choices: 1.

Beef Goulash

*Depending on how much heat you like, choose sweet
or hot Hungarian paprika to spice this goulash.*
SERVINGS 6 (1 cup goulash and ⅓ cup noodles each)
CARB. PER SERVING 27 g

1½ pounds beef stew meat
 2 medium carrots, bias-cut into ½-inch-thick slices
 2 medium onions, thinly sliced
 3 cloves garlic, minced
1¼ cups lower-sodium beef broth
 1 6-ounce can tomato paste
 1 tablespoon Hungarian paprika
 1 teaspoon finely shredded lemon peel
½ teaspoon caraway seeds
¼ teaspoon salt
¼ teaspoon black pepper
 1 bay leaf
 1 red or green sweet pepper, cut into bite-size strips
 2 cups hot cooked noodles
¼ cup light sour cream or plain low-fat yogurt

1. In a 3½- or 4-quart slow cooker, combine beef, carrots, onions, and garlic. In a small bowl, combine broth, tomato paste, paprika, lemon peel, caraway seeds, salt, black pepper, and bay leaf. Stir into vegetable and beef mixture in cooker.
2. Cover and cook on low-heat setting for 8 to 9 hours or on high-heat setting for 3½ to 4½ hours.
3. If using low-heat setting, turn to high-heat setting. Stir in sweet pepper strips. Cover and cook for 30 minutes more. Discard bay leaf. Serve with hot cooked noodles. Top individual servings with sour cream. If desired, sprinkle with additional paprika.
PER SERVING: 295 cal., 7 g total fat (3 g sat. fat), 68 mg chol., 522 mg sodium, 27 g carb., 4 g fiber, 31 g pro. Exchanges: 1 vegetable, 1.5 starch, 3 lean meat, 0.5 fat. Carb choices: 2.

Beef and Bean Ragoût

Kidney beans are used here, but any bean will do—try Great Northern, cannellini, or even pinto.

North African Beef Stew

Cumin, cayenne, cinnamon, and dried fruits give this stew its interesting North African angle.

SERVINGS 4 (2 cups each)

CARB. PER SERVING 33 g

1¼ pounds beef stew meat
2 medium sweet potatoes, peeled, halved lengthwise, and cut into ½-inch-thick slices
1 medium onion, cut into wedges
1 14-ounce can lower-sodium beef broth
1 teaspoon ground cumin
¼ teaspoon ground cinnamon
¼ teaspoon cayenne pepper
4 cloves garlic, minced
1 14.5-ounce can no-salt-added diced tomatoes, undrained
½ cup dried apricots or pitted dried plums (prunes), quartered
2 tablespoons chopped unsalted peanuts
Sliced green onion (optional)

1. In a 3½- or 4-quart slow cooker, combine beef, sweet potatoes, and onion. Stir broth, cumin, cinnamon, cayenne pepper, and garlic into mixture in cooker.
2. Cover and cook on low-heat setting for 7 to 8 hours or on high-heat setting for 3½ to 4 hours.
3. Stir in undrained tomatoes and dried apricots. Sprinkle individual servings with peanuts and, if desired, green onion.

NORTH AFRICAN LAMB STEW: Prepare stew as directed, except substitute lamb for the beef. For 1¼ pounds lean lamb stew meat, trim fat from a 1¾-pound boneless lamb chuck roast. Cut into 1-inch pieces.

PER SERVING: 340 cal., 8 g total fat (2 g sat. fat), 84 mg chol., 356 mg sodium, 33 g carb., 6 g fiber, 35 g pro. Exchanges: 1 vegetable, 0.5 fruit, 1.5 starch, 4 lean meat. Carb choices: 2.

Beef and Bean Ragoût

A ragoût is a rich, well-seasoned stew. Beans and beef star in this tasty version.

SERVINGS 6 (about 1 cup each)

CARB. PER SERVING 34 g

1 pound beef stew meat, cut into 1-inch cubes
1 16-ounce can kidney beans, rinsed and drained
1 15-ounce can tomato sauce with onion and garlic
1 14.5-ounce can no-salt-added stewed tomatoes, undrained
½ of a 28-ounce package frozen diced hash brown potatoes with onions and peppers (about 4 cups)
2 teaspoons Italian seasoning, crushed
Fresh oregano leaves (optional)

1. In a 3½- or 4-quart slow cooker, stir together beef, beans, tomato sauce, undrained tomatoes, hash brown potatoes, and Italian seasoning.
2. Cover and cook on low-heat setting for 8 to 10 hours or on high-heat setting for 4 to 5 hours. If desired, garnish individual servings with fresh oregano leaves.

PER SERVING: 249 cal., 3 g total fat (1 g sat. fat), 45 mg chol., 527 mg sodium, 34 g carb., 7 g fiber, 24 g pro. Exchanges: 1 vegetable, 2 starch, 2 lean meat. Carb choices: 2.

Burgundy Beef Stew

Burgundy Beef Stew

Burgundy wines are made from Pinot Noir grapes, so if you don't want to splurge for a real Burgundy wine from France, simply choose a good Pinot Noir from California.

SERVINGS 8 (1 cup stew and ⅓ cup noodles each)

CARB. PER SERVING 27 g

- 2 pounds boneless beef chuck pot roast
- ½ teaspoon salt
- ¼ teaspoon black pepper
- 1 tablespoon cooking oil (optional)
- 2 tablespoons quick-cooking tapioca
- 6 medium carrots, cut into 1½-inch pieces
- 1 9-ounce package frozen cut green beans
- ½ of a 16-ounce package frozen small whole onions (2 cups)
- 2 cloves garlic, minced
- 1 14-ounce can lower-sodium beef broth
- 1 cup Burgundy wine
- 3 cups hot cooked wide noodles
- 4 slices turkey bacon, cooked according to package directions and chopped

1. Trim fat from roast. Cut roast into 1-inch pieces. Sprinkle meat with salt and pepper. If desired, in a large skillet, brown meat, half at a time, in hot oil over medium heat. Drain off fat.

2. Place meat in a 3½- or 4-quart slow cooker. Sprinkle with tapioca. Stir in carrots, green beans, onions, and garlic. Pour broth and Burgundy over meat mixture.

3. Cover and cook on low-heat setting for 10 to 12 hours or on high-heat setting for 5 to 6 hours. Serve over hot cooked noodles and sprinkle with bacon.

PER SERVING: 318 cal., 7 g total fat (2 g sat. fat), 92 mg chol., 451 mg sodium, 27 g carb., 3 g fiber, 30 g pro. Exchanges: 1.5 vegetable, 1 starch, 3.5 lean meat, 1 fat. Carb choices: 2.

Paprika Beef Stew

You'll want to use fresh paprika at its peak color. So if yours has been on the shelf at room temperature for more than 6 months, replace it. Paprika and other red spices keep best in the refrigerator.

SERVINGS 6 (1 cup each)
CARB. PER SERVING 15 g

- 2 pounds boneless beef chuck pot roast
- 1½ cups chopped onions (3 medium)
- 1 14-ounce can reduced-sodium beef broth
- 1½ cups water
- 1 6-ounce can tomato paste
- 3 cloves garlic, minced
- 1 tablespoon paprika
- 1 tablespoon caraway seeds
- 2 teaspoons dried marjoram, crushed
- ¼ teaspoon black pepper
- 2 cups coarsely chopped green and/or red sweet peppers (2 large)
- ½ cup light sour cream

1. Trim fat from roast. Cut roast into ¾-inch pieces. In a 3½- or 4-quart slow cooker, combine meat, onions, broth, water, tomato paste, garlic, paprika, caraway seeds, marjoram, and black pepper.

2. Cover and cook on low-heat setting for 8 to 9 hours or on high-heat setting for 4 to 4½ hours. Stir in sweet peppers the last 45 minutes of cooking. Top individual servings with sour cream.

PER SERVING: 280 cal., 8 g total fat (3 g sat. fat), 96 mg chol., 259 mg sodium, 15 g carb., 3 g fiber, 37 g pro. Exchanges: 2.5 vegetable, 4.5 lean meat. Carb choices: 1.

Country Italian Beef

You might want a true soup spoon to eat this flavorful bowl. When a soup is this good, every drop matters.

SERVINGS 6 (1⅔ cups each) to 8 (1¼ cups each)
CARB. PER SERVING 25 g

- 2 pounds boneless beef chuck pot roast
- 8 ounces tiny new potatoes, halved or quartered
- 2 medium carrots or parsnips, peeled and cut into 1- to 2-inch pieces
- 1 large onion, chopped (1 cup)
- 1 medium fennel bulb, trimmed and cut into ½-inch-thick wedges
- 1 teaspoon dried rosemary, crushed
- 1 14-ounce can lower-sodium beef broth
- 1 cup dry red wine or lower-sodium beef broth
- 1 6-ounce can tomato paste
- 2 tablespoons quick-cooking tapioca
- ½ teaspoon black pepper
- 4 cloves garlic, minced
- 1 to 2 cups fresh basil leaves, spinach leaves, or torn escarole

1. Trim fat from roast. Cut roast into 2-inch pieces; set aside. In a 4- to 5-quart slow cooker, combine potatoes, carrots, onion, and fennel. Add meat to cooker; sprinkle with rosemary.

2. In a medium bowl, whisk together broth, wine, tomato paste, tapioca, pepper, and garlic. Pour over all in cooker.

3. Cover and cook on low-heat setting for 8 to 10 hours or on high-heat setting for 4 to 5 hours. Stir in basil just before serving.

PER SERVING: 325 cal., 6 g total fat (2 g sat. fat), 89 mg chol., 485 mg sodium, 25 g carb., 4 g fiber, 36 g pro. Exchanges: 1 vegetable, 1 starch, 4 lean meat, 1 fat. Carb choices: 1.5.

Country Italian Beef

Beef-Vegetable Soup

On a superbusy day, start this soup simmering before you leave home. It will be ready to serve when dinnertime rolls around.

SERVINGS 4 (2 cups each)

CARB. PER SERVING 30 g

- 1 pound boneless beef chuck roast, cut into 1-inch pieces
- 1 tablespoon cooking oil
- 2 14.5-ounce cans no-salt-added diced tomatoes, undrained
- 1 cup water
- 2 small potatoes, cut into ½-inch cubes
- 3 medium carrots, sliced (1½ cups)
- 1 large onion, chopped (1 cup)
- ½ teaspoon salt
- ½ teaspoon dried thyme, crushed
- ½ cup frozen peas, thawed
  Fresh Italian (flat-leaf) parsley sprigs

1. In a large skillet, brown meat in hot oil over medium-high heat. Transfer meat to a 3½- to 4½-quart slow cooker. Add undrained tomatoes, the water, potatoes, carrots, onion, salt, and thyme to cooker.
2. Cover and cook on low-heat setting for 8 to 10 hours or on high-heat setting for 4 or 5 hours. Stir in peas. Garnish with parsley.
PER SERVING: 314 cal., 8 g total fat (2 g sat. fat), 50 mg chol., 517 mg sodium, 30 g carb., 7 g fiber, 30 g pro. Exchanges: 2 vegetable, 1 starch, 3.5 lean meat, 0.5 fat. Carb choices: 2.

Spaghetti-Lover's Soup

Working a few more whole grains into your meal plan makes good health sense. One easy way is to switch from regular pasta to a whole wheat or multigrain variety.

SERVINGS 6 (about 1 cup each)

CARB. PER SERVING 27 g

- 1 pound lean ground beef
- 1 medium onion, chopped (½ cup)
- 1 small green sweet pepper, chopped (½ cup)
- 1 stalk celery, chopped (½ cup)
- 1 medium carrot, chopped (½ cup)
- 2 cloves garlic, minced
- 2 14.5-ounce cans no-salt-added diced tomatoes, undrained
- 1 14-ounce jar spaghetti sauce
- 1 cup water
- 1 tablespoon quick-cooking tapioca, crushed
- ½ teaspoon dried Italian seasoning, crushed
- ¼ teaspoon salt
- ¼ teaspoon black pepper
- ⅛ teaspoon cayenne pepper
- 2 ounces dried spaghetti, broken into 2-inch pieces

1. In a large skillet, cook ground beef, onion, sweet pepper, celery, carrot, and garlic over medium heat until meat is browned and vegetables are tender. Drain off fat. Transfer meat mixture to a 3½- or 4-quart slow cooker. Stir in undrained tomatoes, spaghetti sauce, water, tapioca, Italian seasoning, salt, black pepper, and cayenne pepper.
2. Cover and cook on low-heat setting for 8 to 10 hours or on high-heat setting for 4 to 5 hours.
3. If using low-heat setting, turn to high-heat setting. Stir in spaghetti. Cover and cook for 15 to 20 minutes more or until pasta is tender.
PER SERVING: 252 cal., 8 g total fat (3 g sat. fat), 49 mg chol., 529 mg sodium, 27 g carb., 5 g fiber, 19 g pro. Exchanges: 2 vegetable, 1 starch, 2 lean meat, 0.5 fat. Carb choices: 2.

Spaghetti-Lover's Soup

Pork and Edamame Soup

Eat this Asian-influenced soup with good taste— and nutrition—in mind. Green soybeans (edamame) are a good source of soy, which is associated with a reduced risk of some types of cancer and the maintenance or improvement of bone health.

SERVINGS 8 (about 1 cup each)

CARB. PER SERVING 16 g

- 2 pounds boneless pork shoulder roast
- 1 tablespoon cooking oil
- 2 14-ounce cans reduced-sodium chicken broth
- 1 12-ounce package frozen unshelled green soybeans (edamame)
- 1 8-ounce can sliced water chestnuts, drained
- 1 large red sweet pepper, chopped (1 cup)
- 2 tablespoons reduced-sodium soy sauce
- 1 tablespoon bottled hoisin sauce
- 2 teaspoons grated fresh ginger
- ¼ to ½ teaspoon crushed red pepper
- 6 cloves garlic, minced (1 tablespoon)
- 1 3-ounce package dried ramen noodles, broken
- 2 green onions, sliced (¼ cup)

1. Trim fat from roast. Cut roast into 1-inch pieces. In a large skillet, brown meat, half at a time, in hot oil over medium-high heat. Drain off fat.

2. Transfer meat to a 3½- to 4½-quart slow cooker. Stir in broth, soybeans, water chestnuts, sweet pepper, soy sauce, hoisin sauce, ginger, crushed red pepper, and garlic.

3. Cover and cook on low-heat setting for 7 to 8 hours or on high-heat setting for 3½ to 4 hours. Skim off fat. Stir in ramen noodles (discard seasoning packet). Cover and cook for 5 minutes more. Top individual servings with sliced green onions.

PER SERVING: 307 cal., 13 g total fat (4 g sat. fat), 73 mg chol., 531 mg sodium, 16 g carb., 3 g fiber, 31 g pro. Exchanges: 1 starch, 4 lean meat, 1 fat. Carb choices: 1.

Pork and Edamame Soup

Sometimes you can't be picky about size—if the pork shoulder roast you purchase is larger than you need, freeze the extra for another use.

Pork and Lentil Cassoulet

By substituting brown lentils for the white beans traditionally used in a French cassoulet, you skip the step of precooking and soaking the dried beans. Just add the lentils to the slow cooker straight from the package.

SERVINGS 6 (about 1 cup each)
CARB. PER SERVING 25 g

- 1 pound boneless pork shoulder roast
- 1 large onion, cut into wedges
- 2 cloves garlic, minced
- 1 tablespoon cooking oil
- 2½ cups lower-sodium beef broth
- 1 14.5-ounce can diced tomatoes, undrained
- 4 medium carrots and/or parsnips, cut into ½-inch pieces
- 2 stalks celery, thinly sliced (1 cup)
- ¾ cup brown lentils, rinsed and drained
- 1 teaspoon dried rosemary, crushed
- ¼ teaspoon black pepper
- ⅛ teaspoon salt
- Fresh rosemary sprigs (optional)

1. Trim fat from roast. Cut roast into ¾-inch pieces. In a very large skillet, cook meat, onion, and garlic in hot oil over medium-high heat until meat is browned. Drain off fat.

2. Transfer meat mixture to a 3½- or 4-quart slow cooker. Stir in broth, undrained tomatoes, carrots and/or parsnips, celery, lentils, rosemary, pepper, and salt.

3. Cover and cook on low-heat setting for 10 to 12 hours or on high-heat setting for 4½ to 5½ hours. If desired, garnish with rosemary sprigs.

PER SERVING: 262 cal., 7 g total fat (2 g sat. fat), 49 mg chol., 447 mg sodium, 25 g carb., 9 g fiber, 23 g pro. Exchanges: 1 vegetable, 1 starch, 2.5 lean meat, 1 fat. Carb choices: 1.5.

Pork and Red Pepper Soup

Balsamic vinegar and roasted red peppers add an upscale Italian angle to this trendy soup. Both ingredients were once hard to find but are now widely available.

SERVINGS 6 (1½ cups each)
CARB. PER SERVING 12 g

- 1½ pounds boneless pork shoulder roast
- 1 14-ounce can lower-sodium beef broth
- 1 14.5-ounce can diced tomatoes with basil, oregano, and garlic, undrained
- 1¾ cups water
- 1 cup bottled roasted red sweet peppers, drained and cut into bite-size strips
- 1 medium onion, chopped (½ cup)
- 2 tablespoons balsamic vinegar
- ¼ teaspoon ground black pepper
- 2 medium zucchini, halved lengthwise and sliced

1. Trim fat from roast. Cut roast into 1-inch pieces. In a 3½- or 4-quart slow cooker, combine meat, broth, undrained tomatoes, water, roasted sweet peppers, onion, vinegar, and black pepper.

2. Cover and cook on low-heat setting for 6 to 8 hours or on high-heat setting for 3 to 4 hours.

3. If using low-heat setting, turn to high-heat setting. Stir in zucchini. Cover and cook about 15 minutes more or until zucchini is crisp-tender.

PER SERVING: 170 cal., 6 g total fat (2 g sat. fat), 51 mg chol., 537 mg sodium, 12 g carb., 2 g fiber, 17 g pro. Exchanges: 1.5 vegetable, 2 lean meat, 1 fat. Carb choices: 1.

Chipotle Pork Chili

Smoky, sweet, almost chocolaty chipotle chiles take this pork chili in a direction different from ordinary chili powder. The spicy flavor tastes mild at first, but it builds as you work your way to bowl bottom.

SERVINGS 6 (1⅓ cups each)
CARB. PER SERVING 32 g

- 1½ pounds boneless pork shoulder roast
- 1 tablespoon cooking oil
- 1 medium onion, chopped (½ cup)
- 1 medium yellow or red sweet pepper, chopped (½ cup)
- 1 to 2 canned chipotle chile peppers in adobo sauce, finely chopped
- 1 10-ounce can diced tomatoes and green chiles, undrained
- 2 15- to 16-ounce cans red kidney, black, and/or pinto beans, rinsed and drained
- 1 cup beer or water
- ½ cup water
- ¼ cup bottled salsa
- 2 teaspoons chili powder
- 1 teaspoon ground cumin
- 4 cloves garlic, minced
- ¼ cup light sour cream (optional)
- Fresh cilantro sprigs (optional)

1. Trim fat from roast. Cut roast into ¾-inch pieces. In a large skillet, brown meat, half at a time, in hot oil over medium heat. Drain off fat. Transfer meat to a 3½- or 4-quart slow cooker. Stir in onion, sweet pepper, chipotle peppers, undrained tomatoes, drained beans, beer, the water, salsa, chili powder, cumin, and garlic.

2. Cover and cook on low-heat setting for 7 to 8 hours or on high-heat setting for 3½ to 4 hours.

3. If desired, top individual servings with sour cream and cilantro.

PER SERVING: 338 cal., 9 g total fat (3 g sat. fat), 73 mg chol., 607 mg sodium, 32 g carb., 9 g fiber, 34 g pro. Exchanges: 0.5 vegetable, 2 starch, 4 lean meat. Carb choices: 2.

Pork Stew with Polenta

Italian seasoning flavors tender chunks of pork with spinach, peppers, and onions in a tomato broth. Spooned over hot polenta and dusted with shredded Parmesan, this stew is a fine one-bowl meal.

SERVINGS 6 (about 1 cup each)
CARB. PER SERVING 19 g

1½ pounds boneless pork country-style ribs
1 large onion, chopped (1 cup)
1 large yellow and/or red sweet pepper, chopped (1 cup)

1 14-ounce can lower-sodium beef broth
1 14.5-ounce can no-salt-added diced tomatoes, undrained
¼ cup dry red wine
3 tablespoons quick-cooking tapioca, crushed
1½ teaspoons dried Italian seasoning, crushed
3 cloves garlic, minced
1 16-ounce tube refrigerated cooked polenta
2 cups torn fresh baby spinach
¼ cup shredded Parmesan cheese (1 ounce)

1. Trim fat from pork. Cut pork into 1½- to 2-inch pieces. In a 3½- or 4-quart slow cooker, combine meat, onion, and sweet pepper. Stir broth, undrained tomatoes, red wine, tapioca, Italian seasoning, and garlic into mixture in cooker.

2. Cover and cook on low-heat setting for 7 to 8 hours or on high-heat setting for 3½ to 4 hours.

3. Prepare polenta according to package directions. Just before serving, stir spinach into stew. Serve stew with polenta. Sprinkle individual servings with Parmesan cheese.

PER SERVING: 288 cal., 9 g total fat (4 g sat. fat), 92 mg chol., 436 mg sodium, 19 g carb., 3 g fiber, 29 g pro. Exchanges: 1 vegetable, 1 starch, 3.5 lean meat, 0.5 fat. Carb choices: 1.

Lentil and Ham Soup

Brown lentils are actually yellowish green outside and creamy yellow inside. Look for them with the dried beans at the supermarket. If you can't find them, substitute yellow lentils—they cook in about the same amount of time.

SERVINGS 2 (about 1½ cups each)
CARB. PER SERVING 25 g

- 1 cup reduced-sodium chicken broth
- 1 cup water
- 1 stalk celery, chopped (½ cup)
- 1 medium carrot, thinly sliced (½ cup)
- ⅓ cup brown lentils, rinsed and drained
- ⅓ cup diced cooked ham (2 ounces)
- ½ of a small onion, cut into thin wedges
- ½ teaspoon dried thyme, crushed
- 1 cup shredded fresh spinach

1. In a 1½-quart slow cooker, combine broth, the water, celery, carrot, lentils, ham, onion, and thyme.

2. Cover and cook on low-heat setting for 7 to 8 hours or on high-heat setting for 3½ to 4 hours. If no heat setting is available, cook for 5½ to 6 hours.

3. Just before serving, stir in spinach.

PER SERVING: 193 cal., 3 g total fat (1 g sat. fat), 15 mg chol., 795 mg sodium, 25 g carb., 12 g fiber, 17 g pro. Exchanges: 1 vegetable, 1.5 starch, 1.5 very lean meat. Carb choices: 1.5.

White and Green Chili

Cilantro and green salsa give fresh appeal to this chili. If you've never had green salsa, you just have to try it! It's made with tomatillos, fruits that look like green tomatoes but have citrus and apple tones.

SERVINGS 6 (1¼ cups each)
CARB. PER SERVING 26 g

1½ pounds lean ground pork
1 large onion, chopped (1 cup)
2 15-ounce cans Great Northern beans, rinsed and drained
1½ cups green salsa
1 cup reduced-sodium chicken broth
¾ cup water
1½ teaspoons ground cumin
2 tablespoons snipped fresh cilantro
¼ cup light sour cream (optional)

1. In a large skillet, cook ground pork and onion over medium heat until meat is browned and onion is tender. Drain off fat. Transfer meat mixture to a 3½- to 4½-quart slow cooker. Stir in beans, salsa, chicken broth, the water, and cumin.
2. Cover and cook on low-heat setting for 7 to 8 hours or on high-heat setting for 3½ to 4 hours. Stir in cilantro. If desired, top individual servings with sour cream and additional cilantro.
PER SERVING: 250 cal., 9 g total fat (4 g sat. fat), 53 mg chol., 581 mg sodium, 26 g carb., 8 g fiber, 23 g pro. Exchanges: 0.5 vegetable, 1.5 starch, 2.5 lean meat. Carb choices: 2.

Curried Split Pea Soup

If your supermarket doesn't routinely carry smoked pork hocks, ask the butcher to order some for you.

SERVINGS 8 (1¼ cups each)
CARB. PER SERVING 40 g

1 pound dry split peas, rinsed and drained
1 pound smoked pork hocks or meaty ham bone
1½ cups cubed cooked ham (about 8 ounces)
3 stalks celery, coarsely chopped (1½ cups)
1 large onion, chopped (1 cup)
2 medium carrots, coarsely chopped (1 cup)
3 to 4 teaspoons curry powder
1 tablespoon dried marjoram, crushed
2 bay leaves
¼ teaspoon black pepper

1. In a 5- to 6-quart slow cooker, combine split peas, pork hocks, ham, celery, onion, carrots, curry powder, marjoram, bay leaves, and pepper. Stir in 6 cups water.
2. Cover and cook on low-heat setting for 9 to 11 hours or on high-heat setting for 4½ to 5½ hours.
3. Discard bay leaves. Remove pork hocks. When pork hocks are cool enough to handle, remove meat from bones; discard bones. Coarsely chop meat. Return meat to soup.
PER SERVING: 282 cal., 4 g total fat (1 g sat. fat), 24 mg chol., 590 mg sodium, 40 g carb., 16 g fiber, 22 g pro. Exchanges: 0.5 vegetable, 2.5 starch, 2 lean meat. Carb choices: 2.5.

Barley-Vegetable Soup

The hardy barley grain adds bulk and staying power to this savory vegetable soup. You'll feel satisfied long after enjoying a delicious bowl.

SERVINGS 6 (1¾ cups each)
CARB. PER SERVING 45 g

1 large onion, chopped (1 cup)
1 medium carrot, bias-sliced (½ cup)
1 stalk celery, sliced (½ cup)
2 cups sliced fresh mushrooms
1 15-ounce can red beans, rinsed and drained
1 14.5-ounce can no-salt-added stewed tomatoes, undrained
1 10-ounce package frozen whole kernel corn
½ cup regular barley (not quick-cooking)
2 teaspoons dried Italian seasoning, crushed
¼ teaspoon black pepper
3 cloves garlic, minced
4½ cups reduced-sodium chicken broth or vegetable broth
½ cup water

1. In a 4- to 5-quart slow cooker, place onion, carrot, and celery. Add mushrooms, drained red beans, undrained tomatoes, frozen corn, barley, Italian seasoning, pepper, and garlic. Pour broth and the water over mixture in cooker.
2. Cover and cook on low-heat setting for 10 to 12 hours or on high-heat setting for 5 to 6 hours.
PER SERVING: 208 cal., 1 g total fat (0 g sat. fat), 0 mg chol., 589 mg sodium, 45 g carb., 9 g fiber, 12 g pro. Exchanges: 1 vegetable, 2.5 starch. Carb choices: 3.

Seafood is usually best when cooked quickly, so that's why it rarely appears in recipes designed for the slow cooker. When seafood is used, it should be added near the end of the cooking time to prevent overcooking.

Clam Chowder

Turn your slow cooker into a chaudière. That's the French term for the large pot in which fishermen once simmered hearty seafood stews. Chaudière is also the word from which "chowder" is derived.

SERVINGS 6 (1⅓ cups each)
CARB. PER SERVING 15 g

- 6 stalks celery, chopped (3 cups)
- 3 medium onions, chopped (1½ cups)
- 2 medium carrots, chopped (1 cup)
- 1¾ cups water
- 1 8-ounce bottle clam juice
- 1 cup reduced-sodium chicken broth
- 1½ teaspoons dried thyme, crushed
- ½ teaspoon coarsely ground black pepper
- 1 cup fat-free milk
- 2 tablespoons cornstarch
- 2 6.5-ounce cans chopped clams, drained
- 2 tablespoons dry sherry (optional)
- 4 slices turkey bacon, cooked according to package directions and chopped
  Chopped green onions (optional)

1. In a 3- to 4-quart slow cooker, combine celery, onions, carrots, water, clam juice, broth, thyme, and pepper.
2. Cover and cook on low-heat setting for 4½ to 5 hours or on high-heat setting for 2 to 2½ hours.
3. If using low-heat setting, turn to high-heat setting. In a small bowl, combine milk and cornstarch. Stir milk mixture, clams, and, if desired, sherry into cooker. Cover and cook for 30 minutes more. Sprinkle individual servings with crumbled bacon and, if desired, green onions.
PER SERVING: 174 cal., 3 g total fat (1 g sat. fat), 52 mg chol., 629 mg sodium, 15 g carb., 2 g fiber, 23 g pro. Exchanges: 1 vegetable, 0.5 starch, 2.5 lean meat. Carb choices: 1.

Seafood and Corn Chowder

Use any flavor of croutons you have in the cupboard as the crunchy topping.

SERVINGS 6 (about 1 cup each)
CARB. PER SERVING 34 g

- 2 14.75-ounce cans cream-style corn
- 1¾ cups water
- 1 large onion, chopped (1 cup)
- 1 stalk celery, sliced (½ cup)
- 1 medium carrot, chopped (½ cup)
- ½ teaspoon dried thyme, crushed
- ⅛ teaspoon black pepper
- ⅛ teaspoon cayenne pepper
- 1 cup fat-free half-and-half
- 10 to 12 ounces cooked or canned lump crabmeat and/or cooked medium shrimp
- ⅓ cup croutons
  Fresh thyme sprigs (optional)

1. In a 3½- to 4½-quart slow cooker, combine cream-style corn, the water, onion, celery, carrot, thyme, black pepper, and cayenne pepper.
2. Cover and cook on low-heat setting for 5 to 6 hours or on high-heat setting for 2½ to 3 hours.
3. Remove mixture from slow cooker; cool slightly. Transfer half of the mixture to a blender or food processor. Cover and blend or process until almost smooth; return to cooker. Repeat with remaining half of cooled mixture.
4. If using low-heat setting, turn to high-heat setting. Stir in half-and-half and crabmeat. Cover and cook for 10 to 15 minutes more or until heated through. Top with croutons and, if desired, garnish with fresh thyme.
PER SERVING: 195 cal., 2 g total fat (1 g sat. fat), 49 mg chol., 616 mg sodium, 34 g carb., 3 g fiber, 14 g pro. Exchanges: 0.5 vegetable, 2 starch, 1 lean meat. Carb choices: 2.

Hot-and-Sour Soup

2. Cover and cook on low-heat setting for 6 to 7 hours or on high-heat setting for 3 to 3½ hours. Gently stir in tuna. Let stand, covered, for 5 minutes.

PER SERVING: 140 cal., 2 g total fat (0 g sat. fat), 24 mg chol., 576 mg sodium, 14 g carb., 3 g fiber, 17 g pro. Exchanges: 1 vegetable, 0.5 starch, 2 lean meat. Carb choices: 1.

Hot-and-Sour Soup

Be sure to use firm tofu; the cubes will hold together better as they simmer in the soup.

SERVINGS 8 (¾ cup each)

CARB. PER SERVING 8 g

- 2 14-ounce cans reduced-sodium chicken broth
- 2 medium carrots, bias-sliced (1 cup)
- 1 8-ounce can bamboo shoots, drained
- 1 8-ounce can sliced water chestnuts, drained
- ½ cup water
- 1 4-ounce can (drained weight) sliced mushrooms, drained
- 3 tablespoons rice vinegar or white vinegar
- 1 tablespoon reduced-sodium soy sauce
- 1 teaspoon sugar
- ¼ teaspoon crushed red pepper
- 2 tablespoons cornstarch
- 2 tablespoons cold water
- 8 ounces frozen peeled and deveined uncooked shrimp
- 4 ounces water-packed firm tofu (fresh bean curd), drained and cubed
- 2 tablespoons snipped fresh parsley or cilantro

1. In a 3½- or 4-quart slow cooker, combine broth, carrots, drained bamboo shoots, drained water chestnuts, the ½ cup water, the drained mushrooms, vinegar, soy sauce, sugar, and crushed red pepper.

2. Cover and cook on low-heat setting for 6 to 8 hours or on high-heat setting for 3 to 4 hours.

3. If using low-heat setting, turn to high-heat setting. In a small bowl, stir together cornstarch and the 2 tablespoons cold water; stir into chicken broth mixture in slow cooker. Add frozen shrimp and tofu. Cover and cook for 30 minutes more. Sprinkle individual servings with parsley.

PER SERVING: 81 cal., 1 g total fat (0 g sat. fat), 43 mg chol., 410 mg sodium, 8 g carb., 1 g fiber, 9 g pro. Exchanges: 0.5 vegetable, 1 lean meat. Carb choices: 0.5.

Manhattan Tuna Chowder

Although this chunky chowder simmers all day, the tuna is added just before serving.

SERVINGS 6 (1⅓ cups each)

CARB. PER SERVING 14 g

- 2 14-ounce cans reduced-sodium chicken broth
- 2 medium round red potatoes, chopped (2 cups)
- 1 14.5-ounce can no-salt-added diced tomatoes, undrained
- 2 stalks celery, chopped (1 cup)
- 1 medium onion, chopped (½ cup)
- 1 medium carrot, coarsely shredded (½ cup)
- 1 teaspoon dried thyme, crushed
- ⅛ teaspoon cayenne pepper
- ⅛ teaspoon black pepper
- 1 12-ounce can chunk white tuna (water pack), drained and broken into chunks

1. In a 3½- or 4-quart slow cooker, combine broth, potatoes, undrained tomatoes, celery, onion, carrot, thyme, cayenne pepper, and black pepper.

Savory Bean and Spinach Soup

Convenience products such as canned vegetable broth, canned beans, and bottled garlic make preparation extra speedy and easy as can be. The slightly bitter taste of fresh spinach adds a lively flavor to this weeknight dinner dish.

SERVINGS 6 (1½ cups each)
CARB. PER SERVING 31 g

3½ cups water
1 15-ounce can tomato puree
1 15-ounce can small white beans or Great Northern beans, rinsed and drained
1 14-ounce can vegetable broth
⅔ cup finely chopped onion
½ cup uncooked converted rice
1½ teaspoons dried basil, crushed
¼ teaspoon black pepper
2 cloves garlic, minced
8 cups coarsely chopped fresh spinach
2 tablespoons finely shredded Parmesan cheese

1. In a 3½- or 4-quart slow cooker, combine the water, tomato puree, drained beans, broth, onion, uncooked rice, basil, pepper, and garlic.

2. Cover and cook on low-heat setting for 5 to 7 hours or on high-heat setting for 2½ to 3½ hours.

3. Before serving, stir in spinach. Sprinkle individual servings with Parmesan cheese.

PER SERVING: 148 cal., 1 g total fat (0 g sat. fat), 1 mg chol., 451 mg sodium, 31 g carb., 5 g fiber, 8 g pro. Exchanges: 1.5 vegetable, 1.5 starch. Carb choices: 2.

Southwestern Pinto Bean Soup

Kick the flavor of this Mexican-style soup up a notch with a sprinkling of cilantro and a squirt of lime juice.

SERVINGS 6 (1⅓ cups each)
CARB. PER SERVING 46 g

2 cups dry pinto beans
2 14-ounce cans reduced-sodium chicken broth
½ cup water
1 large onion, chopped (1 cup)
3 cloves garlic, minced
1 teaspoon ground cumin
¼ teaspoon cayenne pepper
1 14.5-ounce can fire-roasted diced tomatoes, undrained

⅓ cup shredded reduced-fat Monterey Jack cheese
2 green onions, thinly sliced (¼ cup), or 3 tablespoons snipped fresh cilantro

1. Rinse dry beans. In a Dutch oven, combine rinsed beans and 5 cups cold water. Bring to boiling; reduce heat. Simmer, uncovered, for 10 minutes. Remove from heat. Cover and let stand for 1 hour. Drain and rinse beans.

2. In a 3½- or 4-quart slow cooker, combine beans, broth, the ½ cup water, the onion, garlic, cumin, and cayenne pepper.

3. Cover and cook on low-heat setting for 8 to 10 hours or on high-heat setting for 4 to 5 hours.

4. Stir in undrained tomatoes; cover and cook for 30 minutes more. If desired, partially mash mixture with a potato masher, leaving soup chunky. Top individual servings with cheese and green onions.

PER SERVING: 275 cal., 2 g total fat (1 g sat. fat), 5 mg chol., 538 mg sodium, 46 g carb., 10 g fiber, 18 g pro. Exchanges: 1 vegetable, 2.5 starch, 1 lean meat. Carb choices: 3.

Squash and Lentil Soup

Use a sharp paring knife or a vegetable peeler to remove the golden peel from the squash.

SERVINGS 5 (about 1⅓ cups each)
CARB. PER SERVING 40 g

1 cup dry brown lentils
1 pound butternut squash, halved, seeded, peeled, and cut into ¾-inch pieces
2½ cups vegetable broth
2½ cups water
2 medium carrots, chopped (1 cup)
2 stalks celery, sliced (1 cup)
1 medium onion, chopped (½ cup)
2 cloves garlic, minced
1 teaspoon garam masala

1. Rinse and drain lentils. In a 3½- or 4-quart slow cooker, combine lentils, squash, broth, the water, carrots, celery, onion, garlic, and garam masala.

2. Cover and cook on low-heat setting for 8 to 9 hours or on high-heat setting for 4 to 4½ hours.

PER SERVING: 206 cal., 1 g total fat (0 g sat. fat), 0 mg chol., 510 mg sodium, 40 g carb., 15 g fiber, 11 g pro. Exchanges: 0.5 vegetable, 2.5 starch. Carb choices: 2.5.

Pumpkin, Chickpea,
and Red Lentil Stew

Pumpkin, Chickpea, and Red Lentil Stew

Make this recipe on a crisp autumn day, when pie pumpkins and winter squash are plentiful.

SERVINGS 6 (1⅓ cups each)

CARB. PER SERVING 49 g

1 pound pie pumpkin or winter squash, peeled, seeded, and cut into 1-inch cubes
1 15-ounce can chickpeas (garbanzo beans), rinsed and drained
3 medium carrots, cut into ½-inch-thick slices (1½ cups)
1 large onion, chopped (1 cup)
1 cup red lentils, rinsed and drained
2 tablespoons tomato paste
1 tablespoon grated fresh ginger
1 tablespoon lime juice
1 teaspoon ground cumin
¼ teaspoon ground turmeric
¼ teaspoon black pepper
2 14-ounce cans reduced-sodium chicken or vegetable broth
½ cup water
¼ cup chopped peanuts
⅓ cup plain nonfat yogurt
2 tablespoons snipped fresh cilantro

1. In a 3½- to 4-quart slow cooker, combine pumpkin, chickpeas, carrots, onion, lentils, tomato paste, ginger, lime juice, cumin, turmeric, and pepper. Pour broth and the water over all in cooker.

2. Cover and cook on low-heat setting for 8 to 10 hours or on high-heat setting for 4 to 5 hours. Top each serving with peanuts, yogurt, and cilantro.

PER SERVING: 286 cal., 4 g total fat (1 g sat. fat), 0 mg chol., 617 mg sodium, 49 g carb., 11 g fiber, 16 g pro. Exchanges: 0.5 vegetable, 3 starch, 1 lean meat. Carb choices: 3.

Garbanzo Bean Stew

Garbanzo Bean Stew

Garbanzo beans are wonderfully rich and hearty legumes that make going meatless now and then easy, especially when you pair them with potatoes and just the right spices.

SERVINGS 8

CARB. PER SERVING 51 g

3	15-ounce cans garbanzo beans (chickpeas), rinsed and drained
1	pound red-skin potatoes, cut into ¾-inch pieces
1	14.5-ounce can no-salt-added diced tomatoes, undrained
1	medium red sweet pepper, chopped (¾ cup)
1	medium onion, chopped (½ cup)
3	cloves garlic, minced
2	teaspoons cumin seeds, toasted (see tip, page 127)
½	teaspoon paprika
¼	teaspoon cayenne pepper
2¼	cups water
1¼	cups vegetable broth

1. In a 5- or 6-quart slow cooker, stir together garbanzo beans, potatoes, undrained tomatoes, sweet pepper, onion, garlic, 1 teaspoon of the cumin seeds, paprika, and cayenne pepper. Pour the water and broth over mixture in cooker.

2. Cover and cook on low-heat setting for 9 to 10 hours or on high-heat setting for 4½ to 5 hours. Sprinkle each serving with some of the remaining cumin seeds.
PER SERVING: 258 cal., 2 g total fat (0 g sat. fat), 0 mg chol., 652 mg sodium, 51 g carb., 10 g fiber, 10 g pro. Exchanges: 0.5 vegetable, 3 starch. Carb choices: 3.5.

Cajun-Seasoned Vegetarian Gumbo

With its people-pleasing melange of Cajun seasoning, black beans, sweet peppers, and okra, this zesty gumbo is a cut above the rest.

SERVINGS 6

CARB. PER SERVING 33 g

2	15-ounce cans black beans, rinsed and drained
2	14.5-ounce cans no-salt-added diced tomatoes, undrained
1	16-ounce package frozen stir-fry vegetables (green, red, and yellow sweet peppers and onions)
2	cups frozen cut okra
1½	teaspoons Cajun seasoning
2	cups hot cooked brown rice (optional)

1. In a 3½- or 4½-quart slow cooker, combine beans, undrained tomatoes, frozen stir-fry vegetables, frozen okra, and Cajun seasoning.

2. Cover and cook on low-heat setting for 6 to 8 hours or on high-heat setting for 3 to 4 hours. If desired, serve over hot cooked rice.

PER SERVING: 153 cal., 0 g total fat, 0 mg chol., 470 mg sodium, 33 g carb., 11 g fiber, 12 g pro. Exchanges: 2 vegetable, 1 starch, 1 lean meat. Carb choices: 2.

White Bean and Cumin Chili

Toasting the cumin seeds brings out their deep, nutty flavor. You'll know the cumin is ready when your kitchen is consumed with a deep, fragrant aroma.

SERVINGS 6 (about 1½ cups each)
CARB. PER SERVING 28 g

- 2 19-ounce cans cannellini beans (white kidney beans), rinsed and drained
- 2 14.5-ounce cans no-salt-added diced tomatoes, undrained
- 1½ cups peeled, seeded, and coarsely chopped butternut squash (about 12 ounces)
- 3 medium onions, chopped (1½ cups)
- 1 12-ounce can light beer
- 1 chipotle pepper in adobo sauce, finely chopped
- 1 tablespoon cumin seeds, toasted and ground*
- 3 cloves garlic, minced
- ½ teaspoon salt
- ⅓ cup light sour cream
- 2 tablespoons lime juice
- 1 tablespoon snipped fresh chives
- Small lime wedges (optional)

1. In 3½- to 4-quart slow cooker, combine drained beans, undrained tomatoes, the squash, onions, beer, chipotle pepper, cumin, garlic, and salt.

2. Cover and cook on low-heat setting for 8 to 9 hours or on high-heat setting for 4 to 4½ hours.

3. In a small bowl, combine sour cream, lime juice, and chives. Spoon chili into bowls; top with sour cream mixture. If desired, garnish with lime wedges.

*TEST KITCHEN TIP: To toast cumin seeds, place cumin in a dry skillet over medium heat. Cook for 2 to 3 minutes or until cumin becomes fragrant, shaking skillet occasionally. (Avoid overcooking, which can make cumin seeds bitter.) Remove from heat. To grind seeds, allow to cool. Crush with a mortar and pestle or in a blender.

PER SERVING: 140 cal., 1 g total fat (1 g sat. fat), 4 mg chol., 406 mg sodium, 28 g carb., 7 g fiber, 7 g pro. Exchanges: 1 vegetable, 1.5 starch. Carb choices: 2.

For a tasty soup topper that won't add a lot of carbs, try a spoonful of light sour cream or yogurt, a pinch of fresh herbs, or a sprinkling of cheese.

White Bean and Cumin Chili

simple side dishes

Herbed Wild Rice

When you have more to cook than one oven —and one chef—can handle, call on your trusty slow cooker to help you out. Here's an assortment of savory accompaniments, all healthfully balanced and perfectly formulated for a long simmer in the slow cooker.

Herbed Wild Rice

Toothsome wild rice cooks with mushrooms, carrots, onions, tomatoes, and a generous medley of herbs.

SERVINGS 12 (about 1 cup each) to 14 (¾ cup each)
CARB. PER SERVING 28 g

2   cups fresh button mushrooms, quartered
2   medium carrots, sliced (1 cup)
3   medium onions, chopped (1½ cups)
1   cup uncooked wild rice, rinsed and drained
1   cup uncooked brown rice, rinsed and drained
1   teaspoon dried basil, crushed
½   teaspoon dried thyme, crushed
½   teaspoon dried rosemary, crushed
¼   teaspoon black pepper
4   cloves garlic, minced
1   tablespoon butter
1   14.5-ounce can no-salt-added diced tomatoes, undrained
2   14-ounce cans reduced-sodium chicken broth
Fresh rosemary and/or thyme leaves (optional)

1. In a 3½- or 4-quart slow cooker, combine mushrooms, carrots, onions, wild rice, brown rice, basil, dried thyme, dried rosemary, pepper, garlic, and butter. Pour undrained tomatoes and broth over mixture in cooker.

2. Cover and cook on low-heat setting for 6 to 7 hours or on high-heat setting for 3 to 3½ hours. Stir before serving. If desired, garnish with fresh herb leaves.

PER SERVING: 141 cal., 2 g total fat (1 g sat. fat), 3 mg chol., 188 mg sodium, 28 g carb., 3 g fiber, 5 g pro. Exchanges: 0.5 vegetable, 1.5 starch. Carb choices: 2.

Wild Rice with Pecans and Cherries

If you've been invited to a "turkey and all the trimmings" potluck, this autumn-hued rice pilaf will wow the guests.

SERVINGS 15 (about ¾ cup each)
CARB. PER SERVING 27 g

3 14-ounce cans reduced-sodium chicken broth
2½ cups uncooked wild rice, rinsed and drained
2 medium carrots, coarsely shredded (1 cup)
1 4.5-ounce jar (drained weight) sliced mushrooms, drained
1 tablespoon butter, melted
2 teaspoons dried marjoram, crushed
5 green onions, chopped (⅔ cup)
½ cup dried tart cherries
½ cup coarsely chopped pecans, toasted

1. In a 3½- or 4-quart slow cooker, combine broth, uncooked wild rice, carrots, mushrooms, melted butter, marjoram, and ¼ teaspoon *black pepper*.
2. Cover and cook on low-heat setting for 5 to 6 hours.
3. Turn off cooker. Stir in green onions, cherries, and pecans. Cover and let stand for 10 minutes. Serve with a slotted spoon. If desired, garnish with additional green onions.

PER SERVING: 157 cal., 4 g total fat (1 g sat. fat), 2 mg chol., 235 mg sodium, 27 g carb., 3 g fiber, 6 g pro. Exchanges: 2 starch, 0.5 fat. Carb choices: 2.

Wild Rice with
Pecans and Cherries

Barley-Wild Rice Pilaf with Pistachios

To prevent the barley and wild rice from taking a trip down the drain, use a fine-mesh sieve when rinsing.

SERVINGS 14 to 16 (about ⅔ cup each)
CARB. PER SERVING 19 g

¾ cup regular barley (not quick-cooking)
¾ cup uncooked wild rice
2 14.5-ounce cans no-salt-added diced tomatoes, undrained
2 stalks celery, finely chopped (1 cup)
1 medium onion, finely chopped (½ cup)
6 cloves garlic, minced
2 teaspoons Italian seasoning, crushed
½ teaspoon dried rosemary, crushed
½ teaspoon cracked black pepper
2 14-ounce cans reduced-sodium chicken broth
¼ cup coarsely chopped pistachio nuts

1. Rinse and drain barley and wild rice. In a 3½- or 4-quart slow cooker, combine barley, uncooked wild rice, undrained tomatoes, celery, onion, garlic, Italian seasoning, rosemary, and pepper. Pour broth over all.
2. Cover and cook on low-heat setting for 5 to 6 hours or on high-heat setting for 2½ to 3 hours.
3. Remove ceramic liner from cooker, if possible, or turn off cooker. Let stand, covered, for 10 minutes before serving. Top with pistachio nuts.

PER SERVING: 99 cal., 1 g total fat (0 g sat. fat), 0 mg chol., 166 mg sodium, 19 g carb., 4 g fiber, 4 g pro. Exchanges: 0.5 vegetable, 1 starch. Carb choices: 1.

Creamy Wild Rice Pilaf

Served with roasted chicken or broiled salmon and steamed broccoli, this earthy herbed pilaf makes a great side dish for an easy and colorful meal.

SERVINGS 12 (about ¾ cup each)
CARB. PER SERVING 27 g

Nonstick cooking spray
1 10.75-ounce can reduced-fat and reduced-sodium condensed cream of mushroom soup
1 cup uncooked wild rice, rinsed and drained
1 cup uncooked regular brown rice
1 cup sliced fresh mushrooms
1 cup packaged julienned or coarsely shredded carrots
1 stalk celery, sliced (½ cup)
1 small onion, chopped (⅓ cup)

Barley-Squash Gratin

1½ teaspoons poultry seasoning
2 cloves garlic, minced
¾ teaspoon black pepper
½ teaspoon salt
6 cups water
½ cup light sour cream

1. Lightly coat the inside of a 3½- or 4-quart slow cooker with cooking spray. In the prepared cooker, combine soup, uncooked wild rice, uncooked brown rice, mushrooms, carrots, celery, onion, poultry seasoning, garlic, pepper, and salt. Stir in the water.
2. Cover and cook on low-heat setting for 8 to 9 hours or on high-heat setting for 4 to 4½ hours.
3. Before serving, stir in sour cream.
PER SERVING: 143 cal., 2 g total fat (1 g sat. fat), 4 mg chol., 214 mg sodium, 27 g carb., 2 g fiber, 5 g pro. Exchanges: 2 starch. Carb choices: 2.

Multigrain Pilaf
Wheat berries, barley, and wild rice make this dish wholesome, filling, and infinitely interesting.
SERVINGS 12 (⅔ cup each)
CARB. PER SERVING 24 g

⅔ cup wheat berries
½ cup regular barley (not quick-cooking)
½ cup uncooked wild rice
2 14-ounce cans vegetable broth or reduced-sodium chicken broth
2 cups frozen shelled sweet soybeans (edamame) or baby lima beans
1 medium red sweet pepper, chopped (¾ cup)
1 medium onion, finely chopped (½ cup)
1 tablespoon butter
¾ teaspoon dried sage, crushed
¼ teaspoon coarsely ground black pepper
4 cloves garlic, minced

1. Rinse and drain wheat berries, barley, and wild rice. In a 3½- or 4-quart slow cooker, combine wheat berries, barley, uncooked wild rice, broth, soybeans, sweet pepper, onion, butter, sage, black pepper, and garlic.
2. Cover and cook on low-heat setting for 6 to 8 hours or on high-heat setting for 3 to 4 hours. Stir before serving.
PER SERVING: 147 cal., 3 g total fat (1 g sat. fat), 3 mg chol., 272 mg sodium, 24 g carb., 5 g fiber, 7 g pro. Exchanges: 1.5 starch, 0.5 very lean meat. Carb choices: 1.5.

Barley-Squash Gratin
Cut the squash into ¾-inch cubes so they're big enough to withstand the long, slow cooking process.
SERVINGS 12 (⅔ cup each)
CARB. PER SERVING 21 g

1 2-pound butternut squash, peeled, halved, seeded, and cubed (about 5 cups)
1 10-ounce package frozen chopped spinach, thawed and well drained
1 medium onion, cut into wedges
1 cup regular barley (not quick-cooking)
1 14-ounce can vegetable broth
3 cloves garlic, minced
¼ teaspoon black pepper
½ cup shredded Parmesan cheese (2 ounces)

1. In a 3½- or 4-quart slow cooker, combine squash, spinach, onion, barley, broth, ½ cup *water*, garlic, and pepper.
2. Cover and cook on low-heat setting for 6 to 7 hours or on high-heat setting for 3 to 3½ hours.
3. Remove ceramic liner from cooker, if possible, or turn off cooker. Sprinkle squash mixture with cheese. Cover and let stand for 10 minutes before serving.
PER SERVING: 108 cal., 1 g total fat (1 g sat. fat), 2 mg chol., 224 mg sodium, 21 g carb., 5 g fiber, 5 g pro. Exchanges: 1 vegetable, 1 starch. Carb choices: 1.5.

Southwestern Polenta with Corn and Chiles

A nylon slow-cooker liner coated with nonstick cooking spray keeps this puddinglike mixture from sticking to the side of your cooker. Look for the special liners with the other wraps in your supermarket.

SERVINGS 12 ($\frac{1}{2}$ cup each)
CARB. PER SERVING 14 g

- 2 14-ounce cans reduced-sodium chicken broth
- 1 cup shredded Monterey Jack cheese (4 ounces)
- 1 cup evaporated low-fat milk
- 1 cup coarse yellow cornmeal
- 1 cup frozen whole kernel corn
- 1 4-ounce can diced green chiles, undrained
- 1 teaspoon dried oregano, crushed
- 2 cloves garlic, minced
- $\frac{3}{4}$ cup quartered cherry tomatoes
   Fresh oregano leaves

1. In a 3$\frac{1}{2}$- or 4-quart slow cooker, combine broth, cheese, evaporated milk, cornmeal, frozen corn, green chiles, dried oregano, and garlic. Transfer cornmeal mixture to prepared slow cooker.

2. Cover and cook on low-heat setting for 7 to 9 hours or on high-heat setting for 3$\frac{1}{2}$ to 4$\frac{1}{2}$ hours, stirring once halfway through cooking time. Turn off cooker. Let stand, covered, for 30 minutes, stirring occasionally, before serving. Just before serving, top with tomatoes and fresh oregano.

PER SERVING: 111 cal., 4 g total fat (2 g sat. fat), 12 mg chol., 250 mg sodium, 14 g carb., 1 g fiber, 6 g pro. Exchanges: 1 starch, 0.5 high-fat meat. Carb choices: 1.

Succotash

In the heat of summer, keep your kitchen cool by cooking this all-in-one side dish in your slow cooker while you smoke a beef brisket or barbecue a pork roast on the grill.

SERVINGS 12 ($\frac{2}{3}$ cup each)
CARB. PER SERVING 26 g

- 1 28-ounce can diced tomatoes, undrained
- 1 16-ounce package frozen lima beans
- 1 16-ounce package frozen whole kernel corn
- 3 cups coarsely chopped round red potatoes (12 ounces)
- 4 green onions, sliced ($\frac{1}{2}$ cup)
- $\frac{1}{2}$ cup reduced-sodium chicken broth
- 1 teaspoon dried thyme, crushed
- $\frac{1}{4}$ teaspoon salt
- $\frac{1}{4}$ teaspoon black pepper

1. In a 4- to 5-quart slow cooker, combine undrained tomatoes, frozen lima beans, frozen corn, potatoes, and green onions. Add broth, thyme, salt, and pepper to mixture in cooker.

2. Cover and cook on low-heat setting for 7 to 9 hours or on high-heat setting for 3$\frac{1}{2}$ to 4$\frac{1}{2}$ hours.

PER SERVING: 120 cal., 1 g total fat (0 g sat. fat), 0 mg chol., 243 mg sodium, 26 g carb., 5 g fiber, 5 g pro. Exchanges: 1 vegetable, 1.5 starch. Carb choices: 2.

Glazed Carrots and Parsnips

Jellied cranberry sauce makes a supereasy, ultimately tasty glaze for these two basic root vegetables.

SERVINGS 10 (about $\frac{1}{2}$ cup each)
CARB. PER SERVING 25 g

- 1$\frac{1}{2}$ pounds carrots, peeled and bias-sliced 1 inch thick
- 1$\frac{1}{2}$ pounds parsnips, peeled and bias-sliced 1 inch thick
- 2 teaspoons ground ginger
- $\frac{1}{2}$ cup water
- $\frac{1}{2}$ of a 16-ounce can jellied cranberry sauce
- $\frac{1}{2}$ teaspoon finely shredded orange peel
- 1 tablespoon orange juice
- 1 tablespoon butter, melted
- $\frac{1}{8}$ teaspoon salt

1. In a 3$\frac{1}{2}$- or 4-quart slow cooker, combine carrots and parsnips. Sprinkle with ginger. Pour the water over vegetables in cooker.

2. Cover and cook on low-heat setting for 7 to 8 hours or on high-heat setting for 3$\frac{1}{2}$ to 4 hours.

3. Using a slotted spoon, remove carrots and parsnips from cooker. Add cranberry sauce, orange peel, orange juice, melted butter, and salt to cooking liquid in cooker. Whisk until smooth. Return carrots and parsnips to cooker. Stir gently to coat vegetables.

PER SERVING: 115 cal., 2 g total fat (1 g sat. fat), 3 mg chol., 92 mg sodium, 25 g carb., 5 g fiber, 1 g pro. Exchanges: 1 vegetable, 1 carb. Carb choices: 1.5.

Sneak 'Em In

It's hard to eat too many nutrient-rich vegetables. Add more colorful vegetables each day with these clever tips.

1. **Buy** prepackaged veggies to have on hand for easy snacking.
2. **Start** a meal with a tossed salad or hot or cold vegetable soup.
3. **Grill** vegetables aplenty, then eat them over the next couple of days.
4. **Top** a sandwich with cucumber slices.
5. **Add** cooked mushrooms, onions, and/or sweet peppers to meat loaf or pasta sauce.
6. **Snack** on sweet pepper strips or broccoli florets with low-fat yogurt dip.
7. **Explore** options for salad greens. Try spinach, kale, and collards.
8. **Down** a 6-ounce can of vegetable juice.

Succotash

Southwestern Polenta with Corn and Chiles

Caramelized Onions and Potatoes

This duet of sweet onions and new potatoes makes a meal of steaks or chops really sing.

SERVINGS 8 (½ cup each)
CARB. PER SERVING 25 g

- 2 large sweet onions (such as Vidalia, Maui, or Walla Walla), thinly sliced
- 1½ pounds tiny new potatoes, halved
- 2 tablespoons butter, melted
- ½ cup lower-sodium beef broth or reduced-sodium chicken broth
- 2 tablespoons packed brown sugar
- ¼ teaspoon salt
- ¼ teaspoon black pepper

1. In a 3½- or 4-quart slow cooker, combine onions and potatoes. In a small bowl, combine melted butter, broth, brown sugar, salt, and pepper. Pour mixture over vegetables in cooker.

2. Cover and cook on low-heat setting for 6 to 7 hours or on high-heat setting for 3 to 3½ hours. Stir gently before serving. Serve with a slotted spoon. If desired, spoon some of the cooking liquid over vegetables to moisten. If desired, sprinkle with additional black pepper.

PER SERVING: 131 cal., 3 g total fat (2 g sat. fat), 8 mg chol., 133 mg sodium, 25 g carb., 3 g fiber, 3 g pro. Exchanges: 1.5 starch, 0.5 fat. Carb choices: 1.5.

Caramelized Onions and Potatoes

Rustic Garlic Mashed Potatoes

For the fluffiest mashed potatoes, choose starchy spuds such as russets.

SERVINGS 12 (½ cup each)
CARB. PER SERVING 21 g

- 3 pounds russet potatoes, peeled and cut into 2-inch pieces
- 6 cloves garlic, halved
- 1 bay leaf
- 2 14-ounce cans reduced-sodium chicken broth
- 1 cup fat-free milk
- 1 tablespoon butter
- ½ teaspoon ground white pepper
- ¼ teaspoon salt
- ¼ cup snipped fresh chives
- Whole fresh chives (optional)

1. In a 3½- or 4-quart slow cooker, combine potatoes, garlic, and bay leaf. Pour broth over potatoes in cooker.
2. Cover and cook on low-heat setting for 6 to 8 hours or on high-heat setting for 3 to 4 hours.
3. Drain potatoes in a colander over a bowl to catch the cooking liquid. Discard bay leaf. Return potatoes to cooker. Mash to desired consistency with a potato masher.
4. In a small saucepan, heat milk and butter until steaming and butter almost melts. Add milk mixture, white pepper, and salt, to the potato mixture. Add enough of the reserved cooking liquid to reach desired consistency. Stir in snipped chives. Reserve remaining cooking liquid.* If desired, garnish individual servings with whole chives.

*MAKE-AHEAD TIP: If desired, return mashed potato mixture to slow cooker; keep warm on low or warm setting for up to 2 hours. If mixture thickens, stir in some of the reserved cooking liquid to reach desired consistency.

PER SERVING: 104 cal., 1 g total fat (1 g sat. fat), 3 mg chol., 226 mg sodium, 21 g carb., 1 g fiber, 3 g pro. Exchanges: 1.5 starch. Carb choices: 1.5.

Crock-Roasted Root Vegetables

Don't be surprised when you lift the lid off this delicious vegetable blend. If you use red beets, the color will penetrate the other vegetables, making them pink.

SERVINGS 12 (½ cup each)
CARB. PER SERVING 12 g

- 1 pound butternut squash, peeled and cut into 2-inch pieces
- 8 ounces tiny new potatoes, halved
- 8 ounces beets, peeled and cut into 1-inch pieces
- 8 ounces turnips or rutabagas, cut into 1-inch pieces
- 1 cup packaged peeled fresh baby carrots
- 1 small red onion, cut into ½-inch wedges
- 8 cloves garlic, peeled
- 2 tablespoons olive oil
- ½ teaspoon salt
- ½ teaspoon ground black pepper
- Chopped fresh parsley

1. In a very large bowl, combine squash, potatoes, beets, turnips, carrots, onion, and garlic. Drizzle with olive oil and toss to coat. Sprinkle with salt and pepper. Place squash mixture in a 3½- or 4-quart slow cooker.
2. Cover and cook on high-heat setting for 3 to 4 hours or until vegetables are tender when pierced with a fork. Sprinkle with parsley.

PER SERVING: 71 cal., 2 g total fat (0 g sat. fat), 0 mg chol., 130 mg sodium, 12 g carb., 2 g fiber, 1 g pro. Exchanges: 0.5 vegetable, 0.5 starch, 0.5 fat. Carb choices: 1.

If potatoes are done before the rest of your meal, place a clean kitchen towel beneath the lid that covers them. The towel will absorb any condensation to keep it from falling back into the potatoes and making them soggy.

Crock-Roasted New Potatoes

To ensure even cooking, select potatoes that are similar in size. If necessary, you can quarter larger new potatoes.

SERVINGS 12
CARB. PER SERVING 19 g

- 3 pounds tiny new potatoes, halved
- 8 cloves garlic, peeled
- 2 tablespoons olive oil
- 1 tablespoon snipped fresh rosemary or 1 teaspoon dried rosemary, crushed
- 1 teaspoon salt
- ½ teaspoon black pepper

1. In a large bowl, toss potatoes and garlic with olive oil to coat. Sprinkle with rosemary, salt, and pepper. Place potato mixture in a 3½- or 4-quart slow cooker.
2. Cover and cook on high-heat setting for 3 to 4 hours or until potatoes are tender when pierced with a fork.
PER SERVING: 103 cal., 2 g total fat (0 g sat. fat), 0 mg chol., 168 mg sodium, 19 g carb., 2 g fiber, 2 g pro. Exchanges: 1 starch, 0.5 fat. Carb choices: 1.

Hot German-Style Potato Salad

This slow-cooker version of the old-world favorite is ideal for a family get-together. Stirring in the bacon just before serving helps keep it crisp.

SERVINGS 8 (⅔ cup each)
CARB. PER SERVING 31 g

- 2 pounds potatoes, peeled and cut into ¾-inch cubes (6 cups)
- 1 large onion, chopped (1 cup)
- ⅔ cup cider vinegar
- ¼ cup sugar
- 2 tablespoons quick-cooking tapioca
- ½ teaspoon salt
- ¼ teaspoon celery seeds
- ¼ teaspoon black pepper
- 4 slices turkey bacon, cooked according to package directions and chopped

1. In a 3½- or 4-quart slow cooker, combine potatoes and onion. In a medium bowl, combine 1 cup *water*, cider vinegar, sugar, tapioca, salt, celery seeds, and pepper. Pour mixture over potatoes in cooker.
2. Cover and cook on low-heat setting for 8 to 9 hours or on high-heat setting for 4 to 4½ hours. Stir in bacon just before serving.
PER SERVING: 148 cal., 1 g total fat (1 g sat. fat), 8 mg chol., 242 mg sodium, 31 g carb., 2 g fiber, 3 g pro. Exchanges: 2 starch. Carb choices: 2.

Southwestern Mashed Sweet Potatoes

Serve a spoonful of these kicked-up mashed sweets with slices of roasted pork loin or barbecued ribs.

SERVINGS 10 (½ cup each)
CARB. PER SERVING 22 g

- 3 pounds sweet potatoes, peeled and cut into 2-inch pieces
- 3 cloves garlic, minced
- ½ cup reduced-sodium chicken broth
- ½ teaspoon finely shredded lime peel
- 2 tablespoons lime juice
- 1 tablespoon butter, melted
- 1 tablespoon honey
- 1 tablespoon rum (optional)
- 2 teaspoons ground pasilla or ancho chile pepper
- ½ teaspoon salt
- ¼ teaspoon black pepper

1. In a 3½- or 4-quart slow cooker, combine sweet potatoes and garlic. In a medium bowl, whisk together broth, lime peel, lime juice, melted butter, honey, rum (if desired), ground chile pepper, salt, and black pepper. Pour mixture over sweet potatoes in cooker.
2. Cover and cook on low-heat setting for 7 to 8 hours or on high-heat setting for 3½ to 4 hours or until very tender. Mash with a potato masher.
PER SERVING: 105 cal., 1 g total fat (0 g sat. fat), 3 mg chol., 212 mg sodium, 22 g carb., 3 g fiber, 2 g pro. Exchanges: 1.5 starch. Carb choices: 1.5.

Maple-Ginger Sweet Potatoes

*When baked ham or roast pork is on the menu,
cook a batch of these fruity maple-glazed sweet potatoes
to serve alongside.*

SERVINGS 8 (½ cup each)
CARB. PER SERVING 23 g

1½ pounds sweet potatoes, peeled and cut into bite-size pieces (about 5 cups)
2 medium tart cooking apples (such as Granny Smith), cored and coarsely chopped (about 2 cups)
¼ cup dried cranberries
1½ teaspoons grated fresh ginger
½ teaspoon salt
½ teaspoon ground cinnamon
¼ teaspoon ground nutmeg
⅛ teaspoon black pepper
½ cup water
¼ cup light maple-flavor syrup product

1. In a 3½- or 4-quart slow cooker, combine sweet potatoes, apples, dried cranberries, ginger, salt, cinnamon, nutmeg, and pepper. Pour the water and syrup over all in cooker.

2. Cover and cook on low-heat setting for 5 to 6 hours or on high-heat setting for 2½ to 3 hours.

PER SERVING: 92 cal., 0 g total fat, 0 mg chol., 194 mg sodium, 23 g carb., 3 g fiber, 1 g pro. Exchanges: 0.5 fruit, 1 starch. Carb choices: 1.5.

Maple-Ginger Sweet Potatoes

no-hassle party foods

Buffalo Wings with
Blue Cheese Dip

Bubbly appetizers and steamy drinks prepared in a slow cooker help eliminate many of the time-consuming tasks of hosting a party. With the help of this hardworking appliance and these light bites and beverages, you can free up your time to mingle with guests.

Buffalo Wings with Blue Cheese Dip

You're going to need plenty of napkins, so have them handy when serving this supersaucy finger food.
SERVINGS 32 (1 wing piece and about 2 teaspoons dip each)
CARB. PER SERVING 3 g

16 chicken wings (about 3 pounds)
1¼ cups bottled chili sauce
2 tablespoons bottled hot pepper sauce
Blue Cheese Dip (below) or bottled reduced-calorie ranch salad dressing

1. Preheat broiler. Using a sharp knife, cut off chicken wing tips; discard tips. Cut each wing into two pieces. Remove skin from chicken pieces. Place chicken pieces on the unheated rack of a broiler pan. Broil 3 to 4 inches from the heat about 12 minutes or until lightly browned, turning once. Place chicken pieces in a 3½- or 4-quart slow cooker.
2. For sauce: In a small bowl, combine chili sauce and hot pepper sauce. Pour over chicken in cooker.
3. Cover and cook on low-heat setting for 4 to 5 hours or on high-heat setting or 2 to 2½ hours. Serve chicken wings with Blue Cheese Dip.

BLUE CHEESE DIP: In a blender, combine one 8-ounce carton light sour cream; ½ cup light mayonnaise or salad dressing; ½ cup crumbled blue cheese (2 ounces); 1 clove garlic, minced; and 1 tablespoon white wine vinegar or white vinegar. Cover and blend until smooth. To serve, spoon dip into a serving bowl; if desired, sprinkle with additional crumbled blue cheese. Cover and store in the refrigerator for up to 3 days.

PER SERVING: 54 cal., 3 g total fat (1 g sat. fat), 13 mg chol., 192 mg sodium, 3 g carb., 1 g fiber, 4 g pro. Exchanges: 1 lean meat. Carb choices: 0.

Thai Chicken Wings with Peanut Sauce

These little drummettes cook in a marinade-like mixture before being tossed in a smooth peanutty sauce.

SERVINGS 12 (2 drummettes and 2 teaspoons sauce each)
CARB. PER SERVING 3 g

- 24 chicken wing drummettes (about 2¼ pounds)
- ¼ cup water
- 1 tablespoon lime juice
- ¼ teaspoon ground ginger
- Peanut Sauce (below)

1. Place chicken in a 3½- or 4-quart slow cooker. Add the water, the lime juice, and ginger to cooker.
2. Cover and cook on low-heat setting for 5 to 6 hours or on high-heat setting for 2½ to 3 hours.
3. Drain chicken, discarding cooking liquid. Toss chicken with half of the Peanut Sauce. If desired, return chicken to slow cooker. Serve immediately or keep warm on warm or low-heat setting for up to 1 hour. Serve with remaining sauce (whisk sauce if it looks separated).

PEANUT SAUCE: In a small saucepan, whisk together ½ cup creamy peanut butter; ½ cup water; 2 tablespoons reduced-sodium soy sauce; 2 cloves garlic, minced; ½ teaspoon ground ginger; and ¼ teaspoon crushed red pepper. Heat over medium-low heat until mixture is smooth, whisking constantly.

PER SERVING: 101 cal., 6 g total fat (1 g sat. fat), 15 mg chol., 159 mg sodium, 3 g carb., 1 g fiber, 9 g pro. Exchanges: 1.5 lean meat, 1 fat. Carb choices: 0.

Five-Spice Chicken Wings

Five-spice powder is a blend often used in Asian cooking, especially Chinese-inspired dishes such as these tantalizing appetizer wings. Look for five-spice powder in your supermarket's spice section.

SERVINGS 32 (1 wing piece and 1½ teaspoons sauce each)
CARB. PER SERVING 3 g

- 16 chicken wings (about 3 pounds)
- ¾ cup bottled plum sauce
- 1 tablespoon butter, melted
- 1 teaspoon five-spice powder
- Slivered green onions (optional)

1. Preheat oven to 375°F. Using a sharp knife, cut off chicken wing tips; discard tips. Cut each wing into two pieces.
2. In a foil-lined 15×10×1-inch baking pan, arrange chicken pieces in a single layer. Bake for 20 minutes. Drain well.
3. For sauce: In a 3½- or 4-quart slow cooker, combine plum sauce, butter, and five-spice powder. Add chicken pieces, stirring to coat with sauce. Cover and cook on low-heat setting for 3 to 4 hours or on high-heat setting for 1½ to 2 hours.
4. Serve immediately or keep warm on warm or low-heat setting for up to 1 hour. If desired, sprinkle with slivered green onions.

PER SERVING: 32 cal., 1 g total fat (0 g sat. fat), 9 mg chol., 45 mg sodium, 3 g carb., 0 g fiber, 3 g pro. Exchanges: 0.5 lean meat. Carb choices: 0.

Party Pleasers

You don't have to spend hours in the kitchen to pull together a great appetizer spread. Start with a recipe or two, and fill in with other quick-to-fix items.

1. **Skewer** whole strawberries and cheese cubes.

2. **Wrap** very thin slices of turkey or other meat around chilled cooked asparagus spears.

3. **Serve** vegetable crudités with low-fat dip or dressing.

4. **Pair** low-fat pretzels with spicy mustard for dipping.

5. **Pop** open a can of smoked almonds or other nuts.

6. **Arrange** a platter of cheese and serve with whole grain crackers.

7. **Try** flavored hummus with pita chips.

8. **Steam** a bag of frozen sweet soy beans and serve with reduced-sodium soy sauce.

Thai Chicken Wings
with Peanut Sauce

Spicy Mustard Stir-Fry Bites

Spicy Mustard Stir-Fry Bites

*Wrapped and ready, these good-looking,
bite-size fajitas are savory and filling.*

SERVINGS 25 (1 stir-fry bite each)
CARB. PER SERVING 4 g

Nonstick cooking spray
1 pound packaged chicken, pork, or beef stir-fry strips
½ cup water
½ cup spicy brown mustard
4 teaspoons fajita seasoning
5 7- to 8-inch low-carb flour tortillas, warmed*
1 cup red, green, and/or yellow sweet pepper strips
Snipped fresh cilantro and/or sliced green onions
(optional)

1. Lightly coat a large skillet with cooking spray; heat skillet over medium-high heat. Add stir-fry strips; cook and stir until browned. Drain off fat.

2. In a 1½-quart slow cooker, stir together the water, mustard, and fajita seasoning. Add stir-fry strips, stirring to coat.

3. Cover and cook on low-heat setting for 6 to 7 hours. If no heat setting is available, cook for 6 to 7 hours. Using a slotted spoon, transfer meat to a cutting board. Discard cooking liquid. Cut meat into bite-size pieces.

4. Divide meat mixture evenly among the warmed tortillas. Top with sweet pepper strips and, if desired, cilantro and/or green onions. Roll up tortillas. Using a serrated knife, cut filled tortillas crosswise into bite-size pieces. If desired, skewer with decorative toothpicks.

*****TEST KITCHEN TIP:** To warm tortillas, wrap tightly in foil. Heat in 350°F oven about 10 minutes or until heated through.

PER SERVING: 51 cal., 1 g total fat (0 g sat. fat), 13 mg chol., 173 mg sodium, 4 g carb., 2 g fiber, 5 g pro. Exchanges: 1 lean meat. Carb choices: 0.

Bourbon-Glazed Sausage Bites

*Full-size light Polish sausage is a great replacement
for the usual high-fat cocktail-size sausages.*
SERVINGS 12 (about 2 sausage pieces each)
CARB. PER SERVING 7 g

- 1 pound cooked light smoked Polish sausage or smoked turkey sausage, cut into 1-inch slices
- 1/3 cup low-sugar apricot preserves
- 3 tablespoons pure maple syrup
- 1 tablespoon bourbon or water
- 1 teaspoon quick-cooking tapioca, crushed

1. In a 1½-quart slow cooker, combine all ingredients. Cover and cook on low-heat setting for 4 hours. If no heat setting is available, cook for 4 hours.
2. Serve immediately or keep warm in cooker for up to 1 hour. Serve with wooden toothpicks.
PER SERVING: 86 cal., 2 g total fat (1 g sat. fat), 24 mg chol., 285 mg sodium, 7 g carb., 0 g fiber, 8 g pro. Exchanges: 0.5 carb., 1 lean meat. Carb choices: 0.5.

Italian Cocktail Meatballs

*These appetizers make throwing a party easy.
Four ingredients and two hours—that's all you need.*
SERVINGS 12 (1 meatball and about
1 tablespoon sauce each)
CARB. PER SERVING 6 g

- 1 12-ounce package refrigerated or frozen cooked turkey meatballs, thawed (12)
- 1/2 cup bottled roasted red and/or yellow sweet peppers, drained and cut into 1-inch pieces
- 1/8 teaspoon crushed red pepper
- 1 cup purchased onion-garlic pasta sauce

1. In a 1½- or 2-quart slow cooker, combine meatballs and roasted peppers. Sprinkle with crushed red pepper. Pour pasta sauce over meatball mixture in cooker.
2. Cover and cook on low-heat setting for 4 to 5 hours or on high-heat setting for 2 to 2½ hours. If no heat setting is available, cook for 4 to 5 hours. Skim fat from sauce. Stir meatballs gently before serving. Serve or keep warm on warm or low-heat setting (if available) for up to 2 hours.
PER SERVING: 79 cal., 4 g total fat (1 g sat. fat), 22 mg chol., 304 mg sodium, 6 g carb., 2 g fiber, 5 g pro. Exchanges: 0.5 carb., 1 lean meat. Carb choices: 0.5.

Hoisin-Garlic Mushroom Appetizers

*Cooked in hoisin sauce with garlic and red pepper flakes,
bite-size button mushrooms pack surprisingly big flavor.*
SERVINGS 10 (1/4 cup each)
CARB. PER SERVING 9 g

- 1/2 cup bottled hoisin sauce
- 1/4 cup water
- 2 tablespoons bottled minced garlic
- 1/4 to 1/2 teaspoon crushed red pepper
- 24 ounces whole fresh button mushrooms, trimmed

1. In a 3½- or 4-quart slow cooker, combine hoisin sauce, the water, garlic, and crushed red pepper. Add mushrooms, stirring to coat.
2. Cover and cook on low-heat setting for 5 to 6 hours or on high-heat setting for 2½ to 3 hours. Using a slotted spoon, remove mushrooms from cooker. Discard cooking liquid. Serve warm mushrooms with appetizer picks.
PER SERVING: 43 cal., 1 g total fat (0 g sat. fat), 0 mg chol., 211 mg sodium, 9 g carb., 1 g fiber, 3 g pro. Exchanges: 0.5 vegetable, 0.5 carb. Carb choices: 0.5.

Hoisin-Garlic
Mushroom
Appetizers

White Bean Spread

Warm or at room temperature, this spread tastes terrific. If you'd like to make it ahead, chill the cooked mixture and return it to room temperature before serving.

SERVINGS 20 (2 tablespoons dip and 2 to 3 chips each)

CARB. PER SERVING 13 g

2 15-ounce cans Great Northern or cannellini beans (white kidney beans), rinsed and drained
½ cup reduced-sodium chicken or vegetable broth
1 tablespoon olive oil
3 cloves garlic, minced
1 teaspoon snipped fresh marjoram or ¼ teaspoon dried marjoram, crushed
½ teaspoon snipped fresh rosemary or ⅛ teaspoon dried rosemary, crushed
⅛ teaspoon black pepper
Fresh marjoram leaves and rosemary (optional)
Whole Wheat Pita Chips (below)

1. In a 1½-quart slow cooker, combine drained beans, broth, olive oil, garlic, marjoram, rosemary, and pepper.
2. Cover and cook on low-heat setting for 3 to 4 hours. If no heat setting is available, cook for 3 to 4 hours.
3. Using a potato masher, slightly mash bean mixture. Spoon bean mixture into a serving bowl. If desired, sprinkle with additional fresh marjoram and rosemary. Serve dip warm or at room temperature with Whole Wheat Pita Chips.

WHOLE WHEAT PITA CHIPS: Split 4 whole wheat pita bread rounds horizontally in half; cut each circle into six wedges. Place pita wedges in a single layer on large baking sheets. Combine 2 tablespoons olive oil, 2 teaspoons snipped fresh oregano, and ¼ teaspoon kosher salt; brush pita wedges very lightly with oil mixture. Bake in a 350°F oven for 12 to 15 minutes or until crisp and lightly browned. Remove from baking sheet; cool on a wire rack.

MAKE-AHEAD DIRECTIONS: Cook and mash beans as directed. Transfer bean mixture to an airtight container and cover. Chill for up to 24 hours. Bring bean mixture to room temperature before serving.

PER SERVING: 77 cal., 2 g total fat (0 g sat. fat), 0 mg chol., 173 mg sodium, 13 g carb., 3 g fiber, 4 g pro. Exchanges: 1 starch, 0.5 very lean meat. Carb choices: 1.

Spicy Tomato Dip

Leftovers? Spread some of this pizza-sauce-style dip on an Italian bread shell, then top and bake as a pizza.

SERVINGS 10 (¼ cup dip and ½ cup vegetables or 3 bread slices each)

CARB. PER SERVING 15 g (with vegetables)

1 15-ounce can no-salt-added tomato sauce
1 14.5-ounce can no-salt-added diced tomatoes, drained
1 medium onion, finely chopped (½ cup)
½ of a 6-ounce can no-salt-added tomato paste (⅓ cup)
1½ teaspoons dried oregano, crushed
1½ teaspoons dried basil, crushed
2 cloves garlic, minced
1 teaspoon sugar*
⅛ teaspoon cayenne pepper
3 tablespoons chopped, pitted ripe olives
5 cups assorted vegetable dippers (such as baby carrots or red pepper slices) or 30 toasted multigrain baguette slices

1. In a 1½- or 2-quart slow cooker, stir together tomato sauce, drained tomatoes, onion, tomato paste, oregano, basil, garlic, sugar, and cayenne pepper.

2. Cover and cook on low-heat setting for 5 to 6 hours. If no heat setting is available, cook for 5 to 6 hours. Stir in olives. Serve warm with vegetable dippers or baguette slices.

*SUGAR SUBSTITUTES: Choose from Splenda granular or Sweet'N Low bulk or packets. Follow package directions to use product amount equivalent to 1 teaspoon sugar.

PER SERVING: 68 cal., 1 g total fat (0 g sat. fat), 0 mg chol., 94 mg sodium, 15 g carb., 4 g fiber, 2 g pro. Exchanges: 2 vegetable. Carb choices: 1.

PER SERVING WITH SUBSTITUTE: Same as above, except 66 cal. Exchanges: 2 vegetable. Carb choices: 1.

Vegetable Chili con Queso

If you're looking for a big, bold, flavor-packed appetizer, this one will definitely fill the bill!
SERVINGS 32 (¼ cup dip and ½ ounce chips each)
CARB. PER SERVING 20 g

- 1 15-ounce can pinto beans, rinsed and drained
- 1 15-ounce can black beans, rinsed and drained
- 1 15-ounce can chili beans with chili gravy, undrained
- 1 14.5-ounce can no-salt-added diced tomatoes, undrained
- 1 medium zucchini, chopped
- 1 medium yellow summer squash, chopped
- 1 large onion, chopped (1 cup)
- ¼ cup no-salt-added tomato paste
- 1 fresh jalapeño pepper, seeded and finely chopped (see tip, page 110)
- 2 to 3 teaspoons chili powder
- 4 cloves garlic, minced
- 3 cups shredded Colby Jack cheese (12 ounces)
- 16 ounces baked tortilla chips

1. In a 3½- or 4-quart slow cooker, combine drained pinto beans, drained black beans, chili beans, undrained tomatoes, zucchini, yellow squash, onion, tomato paste, jalapeño pepper, chili powder, and garlic.

2. Cover and cook on low-heat setting for 6 to 7 hours or on high-heat setting for 3 to 3½ hours. Stir in cheese until melted. Serve immediately or keep warm in cooker on warm or low-heat setting for up to 1 hour. Serve dip with chips.

PER SERVING: 138 cal., 4 g total fat (2 g sat. fat), 9 mg chol., 291 mg sodium, 20 g carb., 4 g fiber, 7 g pro. Exchanges: 1 vegetable, 1 starch, 0.5 medium-fat meat. Carb choices: 1.

Rio Grande Dip

Remove the casings from the sausage links and crumble the meat before cooking.
SERVINGS 24 (2 tablespoons dip and about 6 chips each)
CARB. PER SERVING 12 g

- 4 ounces uncooked turkey Italian sausage links
- ½ of a small onion, finely chopped
- 1 15-ounce can reduced-fat refried black beans
- ¾ cup shredded reduced-fat Monterey Jack cheese
- ¾ cup bottled salsa
- ½ of a 4-ounce can diced green chiles, undrained
- 2 tablespoons shredded reduced-fat Monterey Jack cheese (optional)
- 1 9-ounce bag scoop-shape baked tortilla chips

1. In a medium skillet, cook sausage and onion over medium-high heat until meat is browned, stirring to break up sausage as it cooks. Drain off fat. Transfer meat mixture to a 1½-quart slow cooker. Stir in refried beans, the ¾ cup cheese, the salsa, and chiles.

2. Cover and cook on low-heat setting for 3 to 4 hours. If no heat setting is available, cook for 3 to 4 hours.

3. Stir well before serving. Serve immediately or keep warm in cooker on warm or low-heat setting for up to 2 hours. If desired, sprinkle with the 2 tablespoons cheese. Serve dip with chips.

PER SERVING: 76 cal., 2 g total fat (1 g sat. fat), 5 mg chol., 258 mg sodium, 12 g carb., 2 g fiber, 4 g pro. Exchanges: 1 starch. Carb choices: 1.

Vegetable Chili con Queso

The fruit juices in this ruby-red drink provide just-right sweetness— no need to add sugar.

Mulled Cranberry Punch

Mulled Cranberry Punch

To break stick cinnamon, place it in a resealable plastic bag and gently pound it with the flat side of a meat mallet.

SERVINGS 12 (¾ cup each)
CARB. PER SERVING 17 g

- 1 orange
- 8 inches stick cinnamon, broken
- 8 whole cloves
- 4 whole allspice
- 1 32-ounce bottle low-calorie cranberry juice
- 1 11.5-ounce can frozen white grape-raspberry juice concentrate
- 4 cups water
- Thin lemon slices (optional)

1. Using a vegetable peeler, remove several 2- to 3-inch-long sections of orange peel from the orange, avoiding the bitter white pith underneath. Juice the orange.
2. For spice bag, cut a 6-inch square from a double thickness of 100-percent-cotton cheesecloth. Place orange peel, cinnamon, cloves, and allspice in center of the square. Gather corners and tie closed with 100-percent-cotton kitchen string.
3. In a 3½- or 4-quart slow cooker, combine cranberry juice, juice concentrate, the water, orange juice, and spice bag.
4. Cover and cook on low-heat setting for 4 to 6 hours or on high-heat setting for 2 to 2½ hours. Discard spice bag. Serve immediately or keep warm on warm or low-heat setting for up to 2 hours. If desired, garnish drinks with lemon slices.

PER SERVING: 67 cal., 0 g total fat, 0 mg chol., 29 mg sodium, 17 g carb., 0 g fiber, 0 g pro. Exchanges: 1 fruit. Carb choices: 1.

Spiced Fruit Tea

For a smooth liquid, use a no-pulp orange juice.

SERVINGS 10 (about ⅔ cup each)
CARB. PER SERVING 11 g

- 6 inches stick cinnamon, broken
- 1 tablespoon chopped crystallized ginger
- 4 cups brewed black tea
- 4 cups orange-peach-mango juice or orange juice
- Stick cinnamon (optional)

1. For spice bag, cut a 6-inch square from a double thickness of 100-percent-cotton cheesecloth. Place the 6 inches broken stick cinnamon and the ginger in center of the square. Gather corners and tie closed with 100-percent-cotton kitchen string.
2. In a 3½- to 4½-quart slow cooker, combine tea, juice, and spice bag.
3. Cover and cook on low-heat setting for 4 to 6 hours or on high-heat setting for 2 to 3 hours. Discard spice bag. Ladle tea into cups. If desired, garnish with additional stick cinnamon.

PER SERVING: 45 cal., 0 g total fat, 0 mg chol., 11 mg sodium, 11 g carb., 0 g fiber, 0 g pro. Exchanges: 1 fruit. Carb choices: 1.

Citrus Cider

Citrus Cider

Kids and grown-ups alike love this mildly spiced hot drink. Cut each ginger slice about the size of a nickel.
SERVINGS 13 (about ¾ cup each)
CARB. PER SERVING 27 g

- 8 inches stick cinnamon, broken
- 8 whole cloves
- 3 slices fresh ginger
- 2 quarts apple cider or apple juice
- ½ cup lemon juice*
- ¼ cup honey
  Lemon peel and/or lemon slices

1. For spice bag, cut a 6-inch square from a double thickness of 100-percent-cotton cheesecloth. Place cinnamon, cloves, and ginger in center of the cloth. Gather corners and tie closed with 100-percent-cotton kitchen string.
2. In a 3½- or 4-quart slow cooker, combine cider, orange juice, lemon juice, and honey. Stir to dissolve honey. Add spice bag to cooker.
3. Cover and cook on low-heat setting for 5 to 6 hours or on high-heat setting for 2½ to 3 hours. Discard spice bag. If desired, garnish drinks with lemon peel and/or lemon slices.

*TEST KITCHEN TIP: If you squeeze fresh oranges and lemons for the juice, use a vegetable peeler to cut several wide strips of peel from the fruit, avoiding the bitter white pith underneath. Add the peel to the spice bag.

PER SERVING: 105 cal., 0 g total fat, 0 mg chol., 16 mg sodium, 27 g carb., 0 g fiber, 0 g pro. Exchanges: 1.5 fruit. Carb choices: 2.

Berry-Apple Cider

If you have a mandoline, pull it out to cut paper-thin apple slices for the garnish.
SERVINGS 8 (1 cup each)
CARB. PER SERVING 22 g

- 4 inches stick cinnamon, broken
- 1½ teaspoons whole cloves
- 4 cups apple cider or apple juice
- 4 cups low-calorie cranberry-raspberry juice drink
- 1 medium apple, quartered, cored, and thinly sliced

1. For spice bag, cut a 6-inch square from a double thickness of 100-percent-cotton cheesecloth. Place cinnamon and cloves in center of the square. Gather corners and tie closed with 100-percent-cotton kitchen string.
2. In a 3½- to 5-quart slow cooker, combine spice bag, apple cider, and cranberry-raspberry juice.
3. Cover and cook on low-heat setting for 4 to 6 hours or on high-heat setting for 2 to 3 hours. Discard spice bag.
4. Serve immediately or keep warm in cooker on warm or low-heat setting for up to 2 hours. Stir occasionally. Garnish drinks with thinly sliced apple.

PER SERVING: 89 cal., 0 g total fat, 0 mg chol., 11 mg sodium, 22 g carb., 1 g fiber, 0 g pro. Exchanges: 1.5 fruit. Carb choices: 1.5.

happy endings

Chocolate Bread Pudding

More than a vessel for cooking main dishes, the slow cooker is perfect for making homespun favorites such as bread pudding, fruit medleys, and cobblers. Choose something sweet from this section when you have enough wiggle room in your meal plan for a splurge.

Chocolate Bread Pudding

For a light dusting of powdered sugar, spoon the powdered sugar into a small sieve and gently shake over the top of each serving.

SERVINGS 6 (½ cup each)
CARB. PER SERVING 31 g or 24 g

  Nonstick cooking spray
¼ cup refrigerated or frozen egg product, thawed
¼ cup sugar*
1 teaspoon vanilla
1 12-ounce can evaporated low-fat milk
3 cups dry French bread cubes**
½ cup semisweet chocolate pieces
2 teaspoons powdered sugar (optional)

1. Coat a 1½-quart slow cooker with cooking spray. In a medium bowl, combine egg product, sugar, and vanilla. Whisk in evaporated milk. Gently stir in bread cubes and chocolate pieces. Pour mixture into prepared cooker.

2. Cover and cook on low-heat setting for 3 to 3½ hours or until a knife inserted in center comes out clean. If no heat setting is available, cook for 3 to 3½ hours. Turn off cooker. Let stand, uncovered, for 30 minutes to 1 hour to cool slightly. If desired, sprinkle warm bread pudding with powdered sugar just before serving.

***SUGAR SUBSTITUTE:** Choose from Splenda granular or Sweet'N Low bulk or packets. Follow package directions to use product amount equivalent to ¼ cup sugar.

****TEST KITCHEN TIP:** To make dry bread cubes, cut 3 ounces French bread into cubes (should have about 3 cups). Spread cubes in a single layer in a 15×10×1-inch baking pan. Bake, uncovered, in a 300°F oven for 10 to 15 minutes or until dry, stirring twice; cool.

PER SERVING: 202 cal., 6 g total fat (3 g sat. fat), 9 mg chol., 143 mg sodium, 31 g carb., 1 g fiber, 7 g pro. Exchanges: 1 starch, 1 carb., 1 fat. Carb choices: 2.

PER SERVING WITH SUBSTITUTE: Same as above, except 173 cal., 24 g carb. Exchanges: 1 starch, 0.5 carb., 1 fat. Carb choices: 1.5.

When the cooking time is up, turn off the cooker, lift the lid, and let your sweet treat cool about 30 minutes for a just-right temperature for eating.

Angel Cake with
Cherry Sauce

Angel Cake with Cherry Sauce

Amaretto adds just the right amount of almond flavor to the fruit sauce.

SERVINGS 12 (1 slice cake and ¼ cup cherry sauce each)

CARB. PER SERVING 33 g

Nonstick cooking spray
2 16-ounce packages frozen unsweetened pitted dark sweet cherries
⅓ cup cherry apple cider, apple cider, or apple juice
2 tablespoons quick-cooking tapioca
2 tablespoons packed brown sugar
12 1-ounce slices angel food cake

1. Coat a 3½- or 4-quart slow cooker with cooking spray. In prepared cooker, combine frozen cherries, cider, tapioca, and brown sugar.

2. Cover and cook on low-heat setting for 4 to 5 hours or on high-heat setting for 2 to 2½ hours. Remove ceramic liner from cooker, if possible, or turn off cooker. Let stand, uncovered, for 30 minutes to cool slightly. Spoon sauce onto dessert plates with angel food cake slices.

PER SERVING: 141 cal., 0 g total fat, 0 mg chol., 213 mg sodium, 33 g carb., 2 g fiber, 3 g pro. Exchanges: 1 starch, 1 carb. Carb choices: 2.

Sherried Fruit

Cut the plums into thick wedges so their cooking time is equivalent to that of the apple and pear pieces.

SERVINGS 12 to 14 (about ½ cup each)

CARB. PER SERVING 24 g

1 20-ounce can pineapple chunks (juice pack), undrained
3 medium firm ripe plums, pitted and cut into wedges
2 medium cooking apples, cored and cut into 1-inch pieces
2 medium pears, cored and cut into 1-inch pieces
½ cup dried apricots, halved

Fruit Compote with Ginger

1. In a 3½- or 4-quart slow cooker, combine pears, undrained pineapple, dried apricots, orange juice concentrate, tapioca, and ginger.

2. Cover and cook on low-heat setting for 6 to 8 hours or on high-heat setting for 3 to 4 hours. Stir in frozen cherries.

3. Spoon warm compote into dessert dishes. Top with coconut.

PER SERVING: 124 cal., 1 g total fat (1 g sat. fat), 0 mg chol., 10 mg sodium, 29 g carb., 3 g fiber, 1 g pro. Exchanges: 1 fruit, 1 carb. Carb choices: 2.

Mixed Berry Cobbler

A package of muffin mix cooks into a yummy cakelike topping.

SERVINGS 12
CARB. PER SERVING 31 g

Nonstick cooking spray
1 14-ounce package frozen mixed berries
1 21-ounce can blueberry pie filling
2 tablespoons sugar
1 6.5-ounce package blueberry or triple-berry muffin mix
⅓ cup water
2 tablespoons cooking oil

1. Coat a 3½- or 4-quart slow cooker with cooking spray. In a large bowl, combine frozen mixed berries, pie filling, and sugar. Transfer berry mixture to the bottom of the prepared cooker.

2. Cover and cook on low-heat setting for 3 hours. Turn cooker to high-heat setting. In a medium bowl, combine muffin mix, the water, and oil; stir just until combined. Spoon muffin mixture over berry mixture. Cover and cook about 1 hour more or until a wooden toothpick inserted into center of muffin mixture comes out clean. Remove ceramic liner from cooker, if possible, or turn off cooker. Let stand, uncovered, for 30 to 45 minutes to cool slightly before serving.

3. Spoon warm cobbler into dessert dishes.

PER SERVING: 162 cal., 4 g total fat (1 g sat. fat), 0 mg chol., 116 mg sodium, 31 g carb., 3 g fiber, 1 g pro. Exchanges: 1 fruit, 1 carb., 1 fat. Carb choices: 2.

¼ cup sherry or orange juice
2 tablespoons packed brown sugar
2 tablespoons quick-cooking tapioca, crushed
2 tablespoons butter, melted
¼ teaspoon salt

1. In a 3½- or 4-quart slow cooker, combine undrained pineapple, plums, apples, pears, and apricots. In a small bowl, combine sherry, brown sugar, tapioca, butter, and salt. Pour mixture over fruit; stir to combine.

2. Cover and cook on low-heat setting for 3½ to 4 hours or on high-heat setting for 1½ to 2 hours.

PER SERVING: 117 cal., 2 g total fat (1 g sat. fat), 5 mg chol., 64 mg sodium, 24 g carb., 2 g fiber, 1 g pro. Exchanges: 1 fruit, 0.5 carb., 0.5 fat. Carb choices: 1.5.

Fruit Compote with Ginger

A little bit of ginger goes a long way. Wrap any extra fresh ginger in freezer wrap and store it in the freezer.

SERVINGS 10 to 12 (about ⅔ cup each)
CARB. PER SERVING 29 g

3 medium pears, cored and cubed
1 15.5-ounce can pineapple chunks, undrained
¾ cup dried apricots, quartered
3 tablespoons frozen orange juice concentrate
1 tablespoon quick-cooking tapioca
1 teaspoon grated fresh ginger or ½ teaspoon ground ginger
2 cups frozen unsweetened pitted dark sweet cherries
¼ cup flaked coconut, toasted

Caramel-Spiced Apples

Sprinkle evenly with some of the cinnamon mixture. Add remaining apples and sprinkle with remaining cinnamon mixture. Pour apple juice and lemon juice over apples. Stir to coat apples evenly.

2. Cover and cook on low-heat setting for 2½ to 3 hours, stirring gently halfway through cooking time. Spoon apples and cooking liquid into serving dishes. Drizzle with caramel topping and sprinkle with pecans.

PER SERVING: 128 cal., 4 g total fat (0 g sat. fat), 0 mg chol., 33 mg sodium, 25 g carb., 2 g fiber, 1 g pro. Exchanges: 1 fruit, 0.5 carb., 0.5 fat. Carb choices: 1.5.

Old-Fashioned Rice Pudding

Studded with dried cranberries, plump raisins, or dried cherries, this homey dessert gets a fruity boost to its comforting flavor.

SERVINGS 12 to 14 (about ½ cup each)
CARB. PER SERVING 30 g

Nonstick cooking spray
4 cups cooked rice
1 12-ounce can evaporated milk
1 cup fat-free milk
¼ cup sugar
¼ cup water
1 cup dried cranberries, raisins, or dried cherries
2 tablespoons butter, softened
1 tablespoon vanilla
1 teaspoon ground cinnamon

1. Coat a 3½- or 4-quart slow cooker with cooking spray. In a large bowl, combine rice, evaporated milk, milk, sugar, and the water. Add cranberries, butter, vanilla, and cinnamon. Stir well to combine. Transfer to prepared cooker.

2. Cover and cook on low-heat setting for 2 to 3 hours. Stir well before serving in dessert bowls.

PER SERVING: 178 cal., 4 g total fat (3 g sat. fat), 14 mg chol., 54 mg sodium, 30 g carb., 1 g fiber, 4 g pro. Exchanges: 2 starch, 0.5 fat. Carb choices: 2.

Caramel-Spiced Apples

If you have a melon-baller, use it to scoop out the apple core. It will leave a bowl-shape hole that's perfect to cradle the caramel and nuts.

SERVINGS 10 (1 apple half, 1 tablespoon cooking liquid, 1 tablespoon caramel topping, and about 2 teaspoons pecans each)
CARB. PER SERVING 25 g

1 teaspoon ground cinnamon
⅛ teaspoon ground cloves
5 medium red-skinned cooking apples (such as Rome or Jonathan), halved and cored
½ cup apple juice or apple cider
1 tablespoon lemon juice
⅔ cup sugar-free caramel ice cream topping
½ cup chopped toasted pecans

1. In a small bowl, combine cinnamon and cloves. Place half of the apple halves in a 3½- or 4-quart slow cooker.

Cinnamon-Spiced Hot Chocolate

Go ahead, lift the lid. This chocolatey delight requires whisking the ingredients halfway through cooking.

SERVINGS 12 (about ½ cup each)
CARB. PER SERVING 16 g

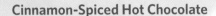

  6 **cups reduced-fat milk**
1½ **cups semisweet chocolate pieces**
  1 **teaspoon instant espresso coffee powder**
  1 **teaspoon ground cinnamon**
    Stick cinnamon (optional)

1. In a 3½- or 4-quart slow cooker, combine milk, chocolate pieces, coffee powder, and ground cinnamon.
2. Cover and cook on low-heat setting for 4 hours, whisking vigorously once halfway through cooking time. Whisk well before serving. If desired, add a cinnamon stick to each cup for a stirrer.

PER SERVING: 125 cal., 8 g total fat (4 g sat. fat), 3 mg chol., 19 mg sodium, 16 g carb., 1 g fiber, 2 g pro. Exchanges: 0.5 milk, 0.5 carb., 1 fat. Carb choices: 1.

recipe index

metric information

The charts on this page provide a guide for converting measurements from the U.S. customary system, which is used throughout this book, to the metric system.

Product Differences

Most of the ingredients called for in the recipes in this book are available in most countries. However, some are known by different names. Here are some common American ingredients and their possible counterparts:

* All-purpose flour is enriched, bleached or unbleached white household flour. When self-rising flour is used in place of all-purpose flour in a recipe that calls for leavening, omit the leavening agent (baking soda or baking powder) and salt.
* Baking soda is bicarbonate of soda.
* Cornstarch is cornflour.
* Golden raisins are sultanas.
* Light-colored corn syrup is golden syrup.
* Powdered sugar is icing sugar.
* Sugar (white) is granulated, fine granulated, or castor sugar.
* Vanilla or vanilla extract is vanilla essence.

Volume and Weight

The United States traditionally uses cup measures for liquid and solid ingredients. The chart below shows the approximate imperial and metric equivalents. If you are accustomed to weighing solid ingredients, the following approximate equivalents will be helpful.

* 1 cup butter, castor sugar, or rice = 8 ounces = $1/2$ pound = 250 grams
* 1 cup flour = 4 ounces = $1/4$ pound = 125 grams
* 1 cup icing sugar = 5 ounces = 150 grams

Canadian and U.S. volume for a cup measure is 8 fluid ounces (237 ml), but the standard metric equivalent is 250 ml.

1 British imperial cup is 10 fluid ounces.

In Australia, 1 tablespoon equals 20 ml, and there are 4 teaspoons in the Australian tablespoon.

Spoon measures are used for smaller amounts of ingredients. Although the size of the tablespoon varies slightly in different countries, for practical purposes and for recipes in this book, a straight substitution is all that's necessary. Measurements made using cups or spoons always should be level unless stated otherwise.

Common Weight Range Replacements

Imperial / U.S.	Metric
$1/2$ ounce	15 g
1 ounce	25 g or 30 g
4 ounces ($1/4$ pound)	11 5 g or 125 g
8 ounces ($1/2$ pound)	225 g or 250 g
16 ounces (1 pound)	450 g or 500 g
$1 1/4$ pounds	625 g
$1 1/2$ pounds	750 g
2 pounds or $2 1/4$ pounds	1,000 g or 1 Kg

Oven Temperature Equivalents

Fahrenheit Setting	Celsius Setting*	Gas Setting
300°F	150°C	Gas Mark 2 (very low)
325°F	160°C	Gas Mark 3 (low)
350°F	180°C	Gas Mark 4 (moderate)
375°F	190°C	Gas Mark 5 (moderate)
400°F	200°C	Gas Mark 6 (hot)
425°F	220°C	Gas Mark 7 (hot)
450°F	230°C	Gas Mark 8 (very hot)
475°F	240°C	Gas Mark 9 (very hot)
500°F	260°C	Gas Mark 10 (extremely hot)
Broil	Broil	Grill

*Electric and gas ovens may be calibrated using celsius. However, for an electric oven, increase celsius setting 10 to 20 degrees when cooking above 160°C. For convection or forced air ovens (gas or electric), lower the temperature setting 25°F/10°C when cooking at all heat levels.

Baking Pan Sizes

Imperial / U.S.	Metric
$9×1 1/2$-inch round cake pan	22- or 23×4-cm (1.5 L)
$9×1 1/2$-inch pie plate	22- or 23×4-cm (1 L)
8×8×2-inch square cake pan	20×5-cm (2 L)
9×9×2-inch square cake pan	22- or 23×4.5-cm (2.5 L)
$11×7×1 1/2$-inch baking pan	28×17×4-cm (2 L)
2-quart rectangular baking pan	30×19×4.5-cm (3 L)
13×9×2-inch baking pan	34×22×4.5-cm (3.5 L)
15×10×1-inch jelly roll pan	40×25×2-cm
9×5×3-inch loaf pan	23×13×8-cm (2 L)
2-quart casserole	2 L

U.S. / Standard Metric Equivalents

$1/8$ teaspoon = 0.5 ml	
$1/4$ teaspoon = 1 ml	
$1/2$ teaspoon = 2 ml	
1 teaspoon = 5 ml	
1 tablespoon = 15 ml	
2 tablespoons = 25 ml	
$1/4$ cup = 2 fluid ounces = 50 ml	
$1/3$ cup = 3 fluid ounces = 75 ml	
$1/2$ cup = 4 fluid ounces = 125 ml	
$2/3$ cup = 5 fluid ounces = 150 ml	
$3/4$ cup = 6 fluid ounces = 175 ml	
1 cup = 8 fluid ounces = 250 ml	
2 cups = 1 pint = 500 ml	
1 quart = 1 litre